The Hitman
The day we murdered God

Editorial Los Bárbaros del Norte
First Edition Copyright 2012
Marcos Barraza Registro en Indautor 2012 oct 3
Losbarbarosdelnorte@gmail.com
ISBN-10:0-9882648-8-9
ISBN-13:978-0-9882648-8-5
Photo Julio Cesar Aguilar Fuentes

Prologue

One of the major issues in the city is the lack of daycares. So, struggling, I built one with capacity for 300 kids.

Specialized personnel ran this daycare, so my main function was to drop by every Friday and pay suppliers and workers.

There it was when I realized that Juarez was no paradise. One day we got a 9-month-old kid with the skin up to the bone and sunken eyes, we took him to the doctor immediately, who ordered lab tests at once. According to the tests, there was nothing unusual about him.

The kid came back and after a month in the daycare his eyes went back to normal and his cheeks regain color, I gathered with the nurse, the director and the social worker so they could explain to me what had happened with this kid.

The answer was simple and plain: "Inge! They wouldn't feed him". In here, a leftist would do a panegyric about poverty from the government, the neoliberal system, from evil rich people who take it all for themselves.

In his file, it said both parents worked, so the nurse started talking about these poor people, so I finished the meeting with a phrase which left them agape: "These aren't poor people, these are sons of bitches!"

Some other occasion I was checking files and one of them caught my eye so I talked about it with the director.

-Such a coincidence that these parents have the same last name –

-No coincidence at all, Inge, they're brothers- she replied.

7

I felt the chills when I saw that the mother was barely 13 years old.

A few days later, when I finished doing the payroll I left, and in the waiting room there was a kid, crestfallen and sad, they hadn't picked him up, it was late and the director was waiting for the mother to arrive.

Trying to distract the kid I came closer and started talking to him.

-Juanito, you were late and now you have to leave late as well- trying to cheer him up.

-We were early, sir, but my uncle arrived and climbed up on my mom- the 4 year old replied.

Not like I'm prudish, or perhaps I am, but his answer left me frozen.

I immediately associated it with all the workers that came all over the country and lived in improvised shacks where, sometimes, a full family lived in just one room. Or both sex worker groups who shared a room, encouraging a huge promiscuity.

That was what wasn't even mentioned in the triumphal factory system speech, the job generator.

As a COPARMEX counselor I attended gatherings with pro men and federal functionaries. Amongst them, there was one particularly that caught my eye due to his harsh speech against the Federation and its great oratorical ability, he described how big Juarez was during the time it was a free zone and he had a personal crusade to restore it.

Curiously, this multimillionaire leader had made his fortune by selling his beer. Workers didn't have to walk that much because in almost every corner there was somewhere they could get a beer or a table dance nearby where they could leave their paycheck.

This was the hero who represented the people. One day, I felt the need to write about all these and sent it to the most popular newspaper, for it to be published. By chance, the person in charge of revising all writings was on a vacation and it was published just as I wrote it. Immediately I received many calls from friends, which were all freaked out: "Don't you know who Freddy is? Do you eat bullets or what? You crossed the line, bato!

Two days later I was called by a friend asking me for a list of the products that were manufactured and distributed in Freddy's stores, I apologized adducing that we didn't have production capacity to provide them. I felt it would have been too aggressive to tell him that what I sold were plastic products, not convictions.

While saying goodbye, he gave me an advice: "don't you ever use names in your articles, we all know whom you're talking about, but they don't feel alluded."

Ordinary people in Juarez have always been characterized by being happy and hospitable, which made that after the crisis there was an astonishing population increase. Many people from around the country would arrive; there was plenty of work for everyone and with better payment than in their original community.

Only the bars and brothels would grow alongside the population, the huge amount of salaries were taken by the vice lords, there were more brothels than schools.

The factory directors would rather cut their own veins, to accept a certain seigneur amongst their directors, line supervisors, managers, etc. with the young town women who came for a fresh start in Juarez.

The number of single mothers increased exponentially, leaving the grandmother taking care of the kid in the best case, since it was the barrio who would take care of them.

Juarez started turning into a city of bastards, in all the extension of the word, kids growing up with no parent authority to guide them, without the presence of a mother and the absolute lack of values.

When the battle for drug control came, Juarez was dry weed, which burned immediately, in terrible proportions.

Sicario kids who showed an unknown fury by then, once I got an email with a picture of a teenager with an AK47 in his right hand and another teenager's head in the other.

The newspapers would report daily extremely violent murders, decapitated, mutilated and burned bodies were spread throughout the whole city and stupid politicians would only say: "It's President Calderon's little war".

Today, Juarez seems to be recovering and we all long for it with our hearts, to be able to see the vigorous and hospitable Juarez again. But just like Albert Einstein said when he was asked to define stupidity, he answered: "stupidity is to do the same and expect different outcomes".

This population must keep an eye on their society model because there is the seed of all the tragedy that goes on, not in external agents.

This book is a compilation of the articles I wrote during this Dante's tragedy.

The Hitman or the day we murdered God

The street is lonely and the wind lifts the dust of sidewalks, people are fearful at home, businesses close and unemployment is rife everywhere.

Some entrepreneurs have been safe in the neighboring country, others migrated south, others of us stayed, perhaps as the wise Greek said: "When death is, you're not, and when you are, death is not, why worry?"

Weekend: 27 dead in 24 hours, new record. Hundreds of small entrepreneurs kidnapped, owners of hardware stores, grocery stores, car washes, doctors, restaurant owners living hell of the uncertainty of tomorrow: entire families plunged into deeper pain you can feel to know that your loved one is in criminal hands.

The media charlatans ask the government for security, so do society, but how to give security?

Putting a policeman for every person will ensure that no one commit crimes?

And is this cop trustworthy or should we also have a cop for him?

We see spectacular crimes, men are beheaded, torn to pieces, mutilated and I would like to ask you about these humanoid beasts that commit such crimes.

What must happen for a normal man to become a beast like these?

Those who have seen these hitmen describe them as young people between 15-25 years.

We all wonder: where is the authority? Why doesn't the president do anything?

And many similar questions, but we do not hear these questions:

Where were the mother and father of these children?

Where were their teachers?

Where were their brothers?

Nobody goes to bed being a good boy and awakens to be a heartless murderer; the transformation is a gradual process.

It's time we stop blaming elsewhere and take responsibility to tolerate a society that grew corrupt and we did nothing to stop it.

"Of course we're not stiff, or retrograde, if the media makes good money by promoting sex. We're already adults; if the boys are breeding out of control it's because we're modern, open minded, bato. What? Do single mothers scare you? Oh, you are a perpetual candle!"

Many women collect children from different fathers and many other men boast and compete to see who impregnates more girls.

Abandoned women who have to appeal to prostitution to support their sons, children growing up with shame of abandonment of their fathers, and occasionally, their mothers.

Women who work and leave their children abandoned, helpless through lust of their neighbors or their own family, irresponsible parents, children growing and accumulating hatred and contempt for society.

We make fun of decency and decorum, we take God out of our schools, our homes, our lives; we eliminate the internal police called consciousness and nowadays, everything is possible, the more depraved, the more in.

The Municipal Public Security Institute of Juarez interviewed hundreds of young offenders, thieves, murderers, rapists and drug dealers, almost all of them came from broken homes and sought acceptance they lacked at home in gangs. Gangs forced them at first to break the law, and then they started enjoying the adrenaline and the feeling of power of dominating another.

It is true that we have a lack of authority. Gentlemen! I must say that authority is born at home Yes, even if you laugh, authority lies within the parents and authority behaviors they should take, lies in morals, in that word so reviled and ridiculed, in the morals, gentlemen.

In morals, in that compendium of good practices that humanity has accumulated over centuries of life, and now thrown down the drain because we're modern. Nowadays the cry of youth is "Let's fuck and shit because the world is going to end" and parents remain impassive and immobile, "don't be afraid, compadre, it's the trend".

The only answer to the serious problem we have today is to return to that compendium of good behavior, to universal values, responsibility, and control of our children, to require the media to stop showing shit on TV, to stop getting our children horny.

Because if we continue allowing single mothers, we'll have to put up with those sons of bitches.

The ideology of death

Each of our actions respond to an idea, explicit or implicit, new or old, nested in the conscious or unconscious, but there will always be an idea beneath our actions.

Countries progress or move back due to ideas; there are dominant ideas, taboo ideas, twisted ideas, fake ideas, but all of them create behaviors.

Good and bad ideas modify the crowds' behavior, this is why it would be interesting to ask ourselves: this evil behavior we see everyday, this violent behavior, is there an ideology beneath them?

I've had a chance to talk with thugs and read their interviews; they always justify their acts.

I've also heard some radical leftists speeches and I find no difference with the thugs' justifications.

Both of them tell us about a class battle between the bad guys, who are the rich, and the good guys, who are the poor, the ones who have everything and the ones who lack the essential.

To all of our red economists the wealth growth is a process of zero sum, this means, for a rich man to be, there shall be a poor, or many.

They yell, they rant against the wealth distribution, they consider that fridges and blenders are given by nature, and when they got there, thieves had already taken them.

This stupidology makes us feel like the poor had been ripped off their wealth and society is in debt with them.

All parties politicians rise this flag over and over again, a project, as dub as it can be, it'll be bless for the poor and every other good project will be attacked. How is it possible that we do this in a 50 million poor country?

Do you remember the dog's tears? "To the have-nots and marginalized, if anything I might ask, it would pardon, because of not letting you out of your sorrow and prostration".

Limitless cynicism, from a guy who looted the country alongside his family and friends, who never assumed any responsibility of his robberies and blamed everyone in the debacle of his six years as president.

Well, now there are poor who are tired of waiting for this promised wealth and who are taking it by their own hand, trough assaults, robberies, kidnaps, extortions and all sorts of thefts – "fucking rich, your time has come".

But, who are these evil rich?

If we go to a low class barrio, the rich will be the convenience store owner, a neighbor who owns a taxi, the blacksmith who just bought himself a truck, the businessman wearing suit and perfume who works at an office. For the storeowner, the rich will be the distributor, for the distributor, the manufacturer, and for the manufacturer, it will be the financier, and so and endless chain is forged, where we all can be the rich or the poor.

This death's ideology, of confrontation, that inflames envy and ambition as main engine of an already sick society.

The ideology which justifies Robin Hood, Chucho el Roto, the one who robs the rich to handle it to the himself, who is the poor.

And don't you think I'm talking about the past in here, this very week the braggart and violent Moreira demands a meeting with Calderon to talk about the way he treated the poor.

This ideology has brought wealth to the poor's leaders. But today, society is paying with their lives and patrimony this speech's debts, nowadays, this ideology is killing us and no one dares to refute it, there's no one who weighs work or effort as a goal towards wealth. He who has must be ripped off possessions; despite they were all earned through the years.

15

I've seen how tough and mature men lose everything they've worked for during their lives because of a kidnap, sinking their family in abandonment and them in the most absolute desperation, I've also heard a leftist troubadour saying that they sought for it, for they were ostentatious.

The classes' battle is the death's ideology; charity is not in a communist manifest, but in the Mountain's Lecture, let's not make that mistake.

We must remove from the collective subconscious all the bullshit left from the leftist speech and we shall rebuild our ideology based in labor and true charity.

The maquila and the droit de seigneur

Visiting Juarez without visiting industrial parks is as good as not doing it, there are elements in the maquila that make us proud. First world factories in nice buildings, well equipped, production lines with international awards, admired technicians, skilled operators, excellent officials that make us exclaim: wow!

But, as they say in my town, 'the whole mountain is not made of oregano'. Bato, the maquiladora scheme has caused serious problems to the city which are not brought up because there is an underground complicity on much of the frontier society.

Back in the seventies William Farber wrote "The Mexican designed by the enemy". It seems like the plan for Mexican maquila came out of this book, the first ones which came were intensive maquilas in cheap labor, and Juarez turned into a magnet of this type of people, who came from around the country to get a job. Some arrived with relatives, others were crammed into small houses, others came with their family and some others, single and looking for an opportunity.

The demand for qualified personnel in Juarez generated universities and tech schools which produced low-cost technicians, the maquila took care of their specialized training in order to take them to a global competitive level.

Female operators were more efficient than male operators, and cheaper , do not ask me why, but this is a reality, payroll money turned out to be an interesting loot for those professional drinkers on Fridays, I'm not going to say names because then Freddy 's friends might get angry .

After and even before meeting the most basic needs, much of those wages stayed in bars and brothels around the city, one would think that two incomes in a family would lead to a better standard of living, but it was not always so, the wide range of these kind of entertainment perverted a large segment of the population.

Pretty girls coming from out of town proved to be a temptation for managers and supervisors who found a modern way of exercising the rights, which is why Yucatecan landlords are remembered for.

Before a year had passed, the girls already had their souvenir, requiring diapers and milk, some returned to the maquila and others opted for a job which paid them what the maquila gave them a week, famous table dances.

Sooner than thought prejudices were put aside and the table dances were all over the city and for all budgets, pornography was broadcast by all media, including television, no one dared to say a thing, "we are really modern".

The women were set free and they even took care of their men, although in different forms than Oaxacan matriarchy, single mothers increased in all social strata and Juarez was flooded with bastards.

Children abandoned by their parents to the neighborhood, relatives or friends, children who grew up without the concept of good and evil, which did not have the signature of a loving, but firm parent hand to correct them, and accumulating all the rancor that forgetfulness and neglect can generate .

Today, amazed we wonder: where do these guys who cut off the heads of their victims come from?

Juarez is the city of the great and beautiful industrial parks, efficient work groups, but also, Juarez is home of abandoned and used women, drugs, alcohol, prostitution , robberies and crimes.

Today, there is a stampede, people are leaving, seems like Evil Juarez is eliminating Virtuous Juarez, don't you think?

Legality or justice

In 1998 there was a survey amongst Mexicans living in the U.S., there were two redundant questions: why had they left? And why they hadn't come back? Everyone would think the answer would be the same for both questions, to find a better pay for their effort; the hypothesis was right.

Most people emigrated to get more money; yet, the surprise came with the second answer, why didn't they come back?

Most answered that it was because they felt safer in the U.S., the survey's analysts were shocked. How could it be that they feel safer in a foreign country?

The filtering of crimes amongst Mexican polices is no secret, newspapers and TV show us everyday policemen and ex policemen as criminals running cartels.

Hundreds of policemen and ex policemen are in jail.

But crime infiltration in the police doesn't stop there, there are facts which let us know that this infiltration exists within the law system, the media also shows us how this criminals are caught, this one confesses or gets caught "in fraganti" and is set free just a few days later so he can go back to commit felonies.

"It's just that the file wasn't well made", is what they say with a ceremonious voice, so we buy it. We live with the fact that the judge let a confessed criminal free because the lazy 345 wasn´t legible or because the ministry agent didn't turn the papers in on time.

It would be good to ask to the judge: Where's the justice? Criteria don't count? Doesn't it make you feel unsafe leaving this criminal out in the streets again? The only thing this judge will do is look up to the sky and say: "it's the law".

We're getting to this terrible paradox where law promotes impunity, where judges have no sense of justice or criteria towards good and evil. Where society is on its own, in the hands of criminals and cartels. That anyone can commit any crime, and in the rare case they are caught, there's a chance the judge, the ministry agent or any other agent might "make an honest mistake $$$" and they would be let free.

This hurts society profoundly, nowadays we see policemen in jail, but we also want to see judges and agents behind bars for complicity felonies.

Good people, working people, the ones who take care of the country, need protection, and they aren't getting any. Trust has faded away and worst of all, there's no hope.

Massacre in Juarez

Once again, young men murdered by young men, 14 until now, 13 are killed in the scene and one more at the hospital; the means, the same sorrow, same riots, but none going deep within the problem.

Authorities, as always, mourning and promising an investigation, well, here we see a change, the governor speaks out and says he'll assume his responsibilities. Public opinion, raised by the media, blames the president. The president didn't foresee this; he's done nothing to stop these tragedies.

Let's see, shall the president follow each and every teenager to stop them from becoming criminals? Impossible, should the president hire a policeman for each young man to stop him from committing crimes? And for each policeman, should he hire another one just to keep an eye on him?

Nature and old wise men in humanity solved the problem by having parents as teenagers' authority and as core of society, family.

Oh! But mexicas intellectuals came along, so did feminists and economical disease of media, promoting sex as it was "let's fuck and shit, for the world is coming to an end", so familiar core was dissolved. Single mothers became movie heroes and started giving birth to bastards in industrial quantities, I know a woman who has 7 kids from different fathers.

Oh! But be careful if you dare to talk about this, for you will irritate intellectuals. Mocho! Old-fashioned! Holly water pisser! Illiterate! And feminists will jump to the jugular. Misogynist! Ignorant! Insensitive!

People! We need to talk about this subject because it has become a life-matter one, we can't have a society of bastards with no control, we have to make these bastards' parents responsible as well as perversion promoters, bar owners, drug dealers, and all those who make profit out of morals disappearance in society.

But first call should be given to these teenagers' parents, to be responsible for their acts and control of their kids, by not doing so; they should be locked up along their criminal sons.

We've seen minors as cartel leaders, murdering, stealing and raping; and when they get caught, they get a minor sentence or are just set free.

This problem goes way beyond polices and politicians, this is also society's problem, as well as families", media's, so what we have to do is ponder deeply away from politics and economic interests. Freddy, stop selling alcohol! CANACO, stop funding black orders!; Municipality, stop authorizing bar openings!; TV, stop broadcasting bullshit!; Parents, take care of your kids, nurture them with values, scold them when necessary; Teachers, guide your students and keep an eye on them, tell parents of any deviation.

This is everyone's problem, but so is the answer.

Roots of violence

Thursday was a busy day, not unlike others, but intense.

Very early I receive a call from a good friend who tells me very scared:

- Marcos, they came to my business to ask for a "cuota" or they kill me. What do I do?

- Think quietly, I would tell you to denounce, but you'll have a high chance to sit in front of a criminal or an irresponsible agent, in both cases your life is in danger.

The other advice would be for you to pay, but it would be like feeding the beast and who knows when you'll get rid of them or when you bother them and have them get rid of you.

The most absurd thing would be that you face them, arming yourself and arming your people, but soon you would end up in jail or in the cemetery.

The other one is to close and get out of the city where you can't be found, because as you said it, they know where you live.

Think calmly, as you say, you have all day to think about it.

At 11 I went to the bank, but there was a police line around the zone, they had killed 3 people, the bodies had been covered with sheets and the curious were whispering, while watching from afar.

After lunch, I returned to work and had to go around because they had just killed the owner of a "yonke" which is one block away from work.

Once I sat down to work, Benito arrived, an old hardworking man, with his face twisted, he had witnessed the murder of the yonkero.

-Inge. Some boys with evil face were the murderers; with fury they shot their weapons, inge, why has God left this city?

- Benito, God has not left the city, we've banished him. First, we took Him out of schools, then our homes and eventually our hearts, it's not evil, it's the absence of good. It's been a long time since we stop looking for him and spots are not to remain empty, the new generations are nurtured by violence, neglect, abuse, sex, alcohol, drugs, what can you ask these guys?

- But for how long, Inge?

- The cup is not full, Benito. We still have lots to see, if we're not added to the list of statistics.

- What do you mean by "still lots to see"?

- You can't solve a problem if you're not going to the origins of it, if you don't assume the responsibility you have; and most importantly, if you don't have the courage to fight for what is right.

As long as we think the solution is going to be given by the government by sending more police and more soldiers, we'll see how violence increases because we've the faint line between being a cop and a felon.

When as a society, we assume our responsibility and realize that there are already too many brothels and saloons in the city, too much sex and violence in the media, too much neglect and abuse with children; when we make a commitment to ensure our children's education in universal values and demand that others do the same, the we will be able to see the light at the end of the tunnel.

But not even this is the solution on the discussion table, as long as we still blame others and posture cynical judges, there will be no solution.

We are a society that missed the sense the smell and we have not realized how rot we are.

What will you be as a grown up? Sicario, dad

The lack of high schools in Juarez makes more than 35% of young people drop out of school after mid school.

An educational company decided to make a market survey to find out what the intentions of children's studies were, and they applied these within boys and Juarez in primary and secondary level, a question was 'what do you want to be as a grown up?' And the surprising answer was "Sicario".

"It was the 15th birthday of his beloved one; he got off his truck with his AK-47 without knowing what was to happen". Narcocorridos have become the preferred music for a lot of teenagers who see their friends with their brand new trucks and their wallets packed with dollars.

For those who are not so young and we are dedicated to trivial things like keeping a family, or a small company, we see with great concern as our customers are closing their businesses and go to El Paso or elsewhere. Some unemployed young men are integrated into the gangs or migrate.

The economy of this city, once progressive and hospitable, is going downhill because of violence, and our youth admires these animals.

F. Nietzsche spoke of the "Eternal Return"; societies do not learn and repeat again and again the same mistakes.

There is a very similar background in the Chihuahua; back in the early twentieth century, in a village in the south of the state, there had been an intense economic and cultural activity, the mines of Parral region produced silver and other minerals, exporting worldwide. They could even afford to mint silver coins to several countries, plantations had a major production, only one of which I have a copy of the sales contract, had over one hundred thousand heads of cattle, 50,000 horses etcetera.

Photos of back then are very descriptive about wealth, their beautiful squares with people dressed in business suit, women dressed in beautiful dresses and children with European outfits, bars with large windows where you could see wines from around the world to parishioners dressed as Europeans.

Bullfighting arenas, lounges where European orchestras were presented, theaters with intense activity, palaces built by Italian architects, German metalworking shops, factories where shoes and even stoves were made.

Department store where I could buy British cashmeres, French dresses, Chinese silks and porcelain.

The big bonanza attracted people from all over the world, who came with their ideas and knowledge and sometimes with their investments, but also the wealth attracts criminals and gangs, rustlers and marauders who plundered and fled to the mountains.

By that time, a murderer who was out of all standards for his bloodlust and cowardice displayed, he waited for farms and ranches to be left without men, so he could rob lonely women, then he buried them alive just to be told where the gold was and hid after killing them with unprecedented viciousness.

When the revolution started, this animal integrated to this movement with his men to fight for "democracy" and Parral suffered the most destructive looting in living memory. Now, Villa kidnapped and killed traders and businessmen, destroying entire productive apparatus of the region, men who had trusted this region fled abroad or got killed and kidnapped by the "Great" revolutionary.

After the revolution, the looting didn't stop and people remained vigilant and warned when his "Dorados" were approaching, with bell ringing people hid, so he wouldn't steal their property and women. I'm talking about the post-revolutionary era. Until a good day, a group decides to confront him and his escort and killed him; people took to the streets to celebrate.

Well this is the story that grandparents tell you as a child, after school, we would run out to the square where former villistas, already old, told stories of revolution where the great hero was Villa and logically in our playground, we all wanted to be Villa and sang the villista songs.

"Carranza has no belly because Villa took it off,
with a sharp knife, he gutted it down. "

There was a crazy elder woman with long, white hair and who, when played with marbles (there was Nintendo back then), she would grab us and tell us not to play. Whenever she annoyed us, we would chase her away and made her leave, screaming incoherently; one day, a neighbor grabbed me by the ear and sat me on the sidewalk, then, she tells me the following story:

-One day, the children of this lady were playing with marbles, when Villa and Fierro passed by.

They say Fierro told Villa:

-I bet I can put a bullet in between the eyes of the kid on the left-, and Villa answered:

-Well, I will put it on the kid to the right-, and both hit the bull eye. When the mother found out, she went crazy out of pain.

I still remember her today with her worn out and shabby black dress, her white hair disheveled, her bony face and bulging eyes.

Over the years, after his death, Villa was no longer the villain and heartless murderer; he became the symbol of Parral. Nowadays, the village festival, a century-old tradition that attracts thousands of people has changed its name to "Jornada Villista", where they pay tribute to this beast.

Maybe in a few years, these thugs, extortionists, murderers and kidnappers who terrorize adults and enchant children, are the heroes for future generations. It has happened once, why can't it happen again?

1810 destroyed the economy and the country is bathed in blood and we commemorate it. 1910 destroyed the economy and the country becomes a blood bath, youth are lying on the battlefield and we commemorate it.

Will history repeat itself in 2010? We'll have to celebrate something in 2110 from this century, right?

Teto Villa and his Nickels

Frequently, in Chihuahua you can see photographs of Villa and his Dorados in restaurants; you can even see that famous photo representing Villa riding triumphantly with the Dorados behind.

Villa has become the symbol of the state, the license plates have his image, many identify with Villa, the dust of time has covered raped women and slaughtered men by these "guys"; in the same way merchants plundered and executed, prisoners used for target shooting, the landed buried alive, executed hostages after ransom, children with their heads crushed by the feet of horses, today nobody remembers that, only the triumphant figure of the caudillo and the Dorados.

Within the current emulous, the figure of Hector Murguía "Teto", classic political character, who after practicing kickboxing goes daily to recruit people to support his campaign for governor with a group of suck-ups that emulate Dorados, even when they don't even look like current nickel.

Cocky, arrogant, claims the town because he's with "the poor", this "closeness" to the poor has made him immensely rich and squanders his fortune on his campaign from his City Hall for years.

Teto bathes from the poor and attack the "rich", with that schizophrenia already known from the history of these Mexica redeemers, he'll sure be governor again and recover more than what has been invested and his suck-ups will be minor governors, equally pushy as their employer and messiah.

The question is: Where was that civil society who managed, risking everything, to oust the nefarious state party? Those men and women who went out to the streets to demanded change?

They seem like the ugly doll, hidden by the corner afraid that someone will see them, defeated by the system, and most tragically, defeated by themselves.

It seems that the manifest destiny of this city and our state is to go back to the thirties, times of chiefdoms, of abuses, looting, crime, in a word, PRI.

We'll have to wait a generation to rescue the gallantry and the pride of this town, which sprung up in the desert and has been able to face all kinds of indignities and calamities.

Democracy and justice

Participation of Marcos Barraza in the Forum of Public Safety and Criminal Justice.

From an early age I have heard that we live in a state of law, and the definition is beautiful.

The rule of law, scholars say, is an institutional system in which law enforcement is submissive to the right, linked to respect for the hierarchy of norms, the separation of powers and fundamental rights of men.

They continue in this fantastic world:

In every social rule of law and state action finds support in the standard, so that state power is subordinated to the legal order, creating an atmosphere of absolute respect for the human being and the public order.

The definition adds: the power must be institutionalized and not personalized; that is, it must be laid within legal and political institutions and not on specific authorities, who are holders of temporary power while lining their office.

Both the legal rules of the respective State, as the actions of its authorities, as they implement such a rule, must respect, protect and uphold the fundamental rights arising from the nature of individuals and intermediary forces that make up the plot of society.

We see on television the judges of the supreme court (SCJN), walking majestically with their bulky bodies covered by togas and speak with an almost divine solemnity, and one can only think, good that we have such bright and honest characters who are never wrong .

This paradise disappears when you have contact with any element of "justice", or face a lawsuit as plaintiff or defendant and enter the swamp slowdowns, of indolence, of servility, arrogance, ineptitude, and corruption, all those characteristics lead to the "rule of law" to be its antithesis.

When one listens to the radio and statistics handlers talk about percentages close to 98% of impunity, you realize that if a perpetrator has little chance of being punished, and that leads him to continue attacking the wholly unprotected society on the ground of facts.

When one talks with the police on this issue, they tell you: - we catch criminals in the time of the crime and submit them to the authorities, but the next day they are set free. – Why do they let them free? – One asks, and the other answers colloquially, - because they give them money.

The biggest problem in Mexico is the incongruity between what we say it is and what actually happens.

Constitution, laws, regulations and procedures have become gibberish, not by mistake, but devilishly premeditated, because our laws have proven through the years that they're not looking to serve justice, but to control and plunder of resources and lives of society.

The more complex and convoluted laws are, the more difficult to comply them, and justice will be in the hands of the authorities, creating the possibility to use them in a discrete way for their interests.

I will illustrate this with an example: let's suppose you want to comply with the laws that I.R.S. make properly; well, then you need to read 16 laws, a code, 2 Bill of Rights and 16 regulations with their current decrees, in addition to memoranda and statements, something like 20,000 pages written in unusual terms, technical pompously called, this leads to the field of helplessness, leaving your fate in the goodwill of others.

But still, if you had the time and knowledge to read and assimilate them, there is nothing that guarantees it is safe, because in many cases, the criteria of the authority will have the last word.

But if the laws are confusing and convoluted, procedures are unbearable and endless; if you apply justice, a trial can

32

go several years of visiting the court with an unprecedented expenditure of time and resources, which would inhibit you in the future to ask for justice in court.

And when you get to the deliverers of justice, the issue becomes deeply terrible because corruption hurts the spirit of he who demands justice and trust vanishes when seeing how the judge is sold to the highest bidder.

Against this background, what could be the right way?

After suffering decades of authoritarian rule and a heroic struggle, we have chosen to follow the path of democracy, and that implies a 180 degrees turn.

First,

Our judicial system should be based on rules of conduct, not obedience; that is, the company must establish what the rules are which must be issued for healthy living, not the state dictating the rules that subjects must obey.

Second,

The Constitution must have the rationale and objectives that mark the course of the nation; and as a waterfall create rules that allow us to achieve these goals.

Third,

Civil society needs to generate the politic system that proposes laws to which one is willing to submit to achieve the objectives of the country.

Fourth,

Once established the laws, appoint representatives to implement and enforce them, even with the use of public force.

Much of the change that the country is experiencing was born in this city due to the effort and bravery of the civil society, which demanded their rights to the end, and hence can also come out the initiative to change the courts, something that the nation requires immediately.

In this movement we managed to introduce in the Constitution of the State of Chihuahua the popular initiative, the plebiscite, the referendum and the revocation of mandate, these tools allow us to transform the medieval justice system in an institution at the service of society.

As long as public safety is designed, operated and supervised by the state we can't say that we are a democratic country. The design and supervision of this should lie with civic organizations such as universities, colleges, neighborhood committees that continually interact with the state proposing solutions and monitoring results.

Similarly, the administration of justice must change, as long as officials or politicians are the ones who appoint judges and agents, we'll remain a country of authoritarian rule; if calling ourselves democrats is what we want, integrity and reputation of the judges must be determined by society, not politicians. It's necessary that these are elected the same way that the functionaries from the other two powers are chosen.

Summarizing, we require:

1. - Clear rules issued by the society.
2. - Simple and firm procedures that allow swift justice.
3. - Judicial authorities chosen by society.

Hello? Hello? Testing! 1, 2, 3! Bah, the lights went out.

Defending Calderon President

Trying to defend Calderon is much like entering a fast track in the opposite direction.

Opposite hordes counter attack hard, all against Calderon.

What we should really defend is the need to confront the drug cartels, with the legitimate use of force that belongs to the State and the support of society who dreams of a country free of so much dross.

Society can't continue to take the place of the spectator in this war because it is the most affected.

The drug cartels were taking full control of our nation. Postponing this war as president Fox did, or ally with them and negotiate as the PRI presidents did was to leave society in the hands of criminals.

It is logical that we are tired of seeing executions in our city, hearing the doorbell or the phone and go on alert, or going out knowing that you run a risk of receiving a stray bullet.

To see how close your customers, how people lose their jobs, as entrepreneurs flee to El Paso; we are sick and tired of that, perhaps as we had never been, we live tense and irritated, but we can't ignore that the main culprit is the drugs and the cartels, although this sounds too obvious, but we need to highlight it again and again, just as drug cartels and their allies highlight it, since this war must have never started.

These criminals don't come from the Andromeda galaxy; they are unfortunately from our society. It's hard to believe that a boy who dares to take the head of a human being has had parents concerned about correcting and guiding him; or a teacher attentive to changes in behavior; or a grandmother who gave him good advices, and behind him, we have the big drug dealers who have gotten rich with such brutal activities, and logically defend their gold mines.

Those dealers are not hiding in caves or underground, they are in the choicest sites of our city and many people know who they are and how they grew in that business.

They are the real culprits of the environment that we are living in, and I don't see in the media anyone denouncing them. Then, we have those who should have fought them, but instead, allied to them, I will cite the case of Ciudad Juarez and local politicians.

How is it to be explained that municipal patrols pass out drugs and lifted people and the former mayor didn't receive any demand by the media, but instead applaud him for everything and look forward to have him back again?

How not to complain to the mayor after him, who realized the misdeeds of these cops did not tuck them in jail and questioned the former president?

But if this is explained in the network of complicity, how can I rate the media that do not report it?

How is it that the current mayor tells international broadcasts about it and local media does not require an explanation?

How to explain the complicity of the current governor with Patricio and Chito Solis, when many people knew what kind of business they were engaged in when they found drugs in their brother's ranch?

Several journalists heard from a deputy governor about linkages of governor Baeza and extortionists. Who said a word about it?

And now, we listen to local media, press, radio and television accusing Calderon for everything.

PUFF! How to rate the media? Brave? Overlapers? Accomplices?

You have the best opinion.

P.S.

And Teto came back despite his predecessor denounced him in US TV, as brilliant municipal president of Ciudad Juarez, reelecting himself, to the astonishment of the few and the apathy of many.

ESTRACA law

A study of the UACJ indicates that there are over 80,000 kids who neither study nor work, and guess what? They have been given a name, the ninis, awesome! There's a new species just like the hippies, Neanderthal man, or perhaps a baseball or football team. Ladies and Gentlemen! The ninis in action! The last link in the evolutionary chain! WOW!

On the other hand we see every day in newspapers, radio and television news about robberies, killings, extortions and kidnappings carried out by boys between 11 and 20 years. Is there any link between ninis and these criminals? Or are these criminals from Mars, Jupiter or Venus?

But how dare you suspect of these angels! Barraza! You're hallucinating, these children do not study or work because they spend their days praying and helping their parents in household chores.

What do you want? Force them to study? Fascists! Son of Hitler! Oh no, I know, what you want is to have them working, you evil exploiter, poor children in the prime of their childhood and you want to force them to work , that's why the world is like this, but we won't allow that, that's why the rights of children exist.

How easy life would be if we were only to decide between good and evil, but the joints put us in the dilemma of choosing between bad and worse, and unfortunately we have no way of measuring the degree of evil .

How many of these 80,000 are committing crimes? 5,000? 10,000? We don't know for sure, what we do know is that is on the rise and many productive lives are blinded by these monsters.

Businesses are shutting down for fear of extortion and kidnapping, lying off thousands of people.

What do we do? Put a cop per nini? Have him by his side 24/7? Let them continue killing?

Here next to Juarez there is a city where if the child doesn't go to school, police calls the parents, and if it repeats, offenders go to jail.

Marcos! Trying to imitate the gringos again? We have another idiosyncrasy.

There are problems that know no borders, neither do the solutions.

We are in the dilemma, either we put these children in control or they'll kill us, simple and plain, if we continue with the stupid interpretation of children's rights, we shall soon fall to their bullets.

Kids have to go to school, go to work or go to prison; there is no alternative to the law ESTRACA (study, work, or prison / EStudio, TRAbajo, CArcel).

The methodology and regulation can generate all the possible, but the lack of this law costs lives every day.

The apprenticeships remained for centuries working just fine, the State should tell these ninis: you don't want to study? Then, you have to work; and employers: Mr. businessman, I'll pay half of his salary. Teach him how to work! I assure you we would have a whole different city.

You don't want to study or work? I'll give you your future now and avoid many unnecessary deaths. To jail! With all your stuff.

In an extreme situation such as the one we are living, we just have extreme solutions or disappear.

MOTION ESTRACA.

Jelipe's ambush

The murder of a group of young people in Ciudad Juarez is undoubtedly a miserable, reprehensible act under any circumstances; executioners do not reach the status of human beings, not even beasts.

The pain of mothers, fathers, family is unimaginable, Juarez's society is shivered, terrified.

It is urgent a deep reflection of the causes that led to this slaughter of young lives that were finished so shortly.

A raw reflection, free of taboos and quotes, where we all reflect and take some responsibility.

The murderers did not come or Venus, or Mars, or any distant country, they are elements of a cluster of people who share a geographic space, which is far from society.

Refugee camp in a country that does not create jobs, that has no ideals or explicit principles, a country that denies the faith of their ancestors.

Of a State that was formed to submit its people, of a political class that through privileges and concessions exploits people educated with lies and simulation.

Of a country which tyranny made become apathetic and resentful, which conforms to disown and throw tantrums but remains motionless to constructive and reconstructive action that the nation demands.

Of stupid people who think that the same actions, the same people, the same system will give different results.

We have spent almost a hundred years with a system born of a state coup, bathing in blood of innocent people, dominating, extorting and when we shake off the monster's head, we eagerly yearn for his return.

It is true that the civil epic of 2000 didn't crystallize in the desired change, the system only lost the visible head, but the shadows were consolidated and reaffirmed.

The Messiah could not handle the package and the people, from his hammock; he saw how the system ridiculed him and joined the ridicule and disrepute to crucify him into disrepute.

The coexistence of the State with the crime was an open secret that the good people transformed into a desire that someone would take on this underground power, whose tentacles debased the population.

The messiah who dares confront the hydra with a thousand heads comes and the system picks a side, and is not the President of the Republic's. The first researches are found in a police that completely served the crime police and those were not guided by themselves and municipal councilors apparently could not be unrelated.

The PRI Chihuahua was no stranger to this, the police and the army found evidence that the people of the former governor of Chihuahua were not immune to crime, his huge fortune amassed in his days as governor, his real power still has in serious doubt his honesty, and there he is free and his crimes, unpunished.

Broadcasts' owners have repeatedly attacked the army, not the municipal and state police. The authorities have given a face of concern about what happens in the state, but under the table, boycotting the president's actions.

This became clear at the meeting that the President of the Republic had in Ciudad Juarez, a fence of 7,000 police officers was formed to protect him. Not even the air wafted, however only two meters from the president appeared a woman, yelling at the president.

How did this woman get there? Many federal employees were not allowed in, in the days before this meeting, the PRI and PRD recruited people in depressed areas and universities to make a "spontaneous" protest against the president. These protests were about a mile away and this lady was just 2 meters away from the president.

The answer is clear and obvious to those who are not easily fooled; this lady could only be there with permission and invitation of local and state authorities.

Local, state, national and international media gave wide publicity to the insults of this woman, no one spoke of the strength of the president, his answer, showing respect to it, his concerns and most importantly, the specific deals that he brought to the city.

The PAN, cowardly as always, made no defense, they left the cheese to mice that were filled to satiety, no one questioned the nature of the murderers, their parents, their teachers, the tribes where they live, and everyone blamed the president, in an intellectual infantilism near idiocy.

Happy PRI, "let them have it, so they learn" PAN don't know how to govern, we are good, we do know how to live with crime.

In this election, when placing a cross in the tricolor circle, perhaps you'll be adding a cross in the cemetery, I know you will say that the PAN have failed to make the change and I agree with you, but Rome was not built in a day and the change will take us generations; but we can't stop living because the system's domination will go AD AETERNUM.

"Todos Somos Juarez" work-tables

Maybe you heard that President Felipe requested Juarez's society to meet in working groups to develop solutions to the serious problem that Juarez is going through.

Enthusiastic about the idea I spent the weekend preparing a proposal and very obedient. Today I applied to work presiding table, obviously, the Secretary of Labor.

Presentations began: the important people, the Presidents of the Chambers, important traders, the rectors of the universities; and after some hours, I got the feeling that I was in the wrong place.

I was told it was a work table to offer solutions, but looked more like a wedding gift table where everyone had a list of what the government should give them, but I did not see the bride and groom.

Carefully, I looked for a Christmas tree, maybe this was an extemporaneous letters to Santa Claus I hadn't noticed.

Hours passed and occasionally I approached the skinny girl in control of exponents, "it's almost your turn", she said politely. They announced the end of the meeting and the skinny girl with a cute smile told me that, unfortunately, the time was up, I was going to ask if there was a table where they offered solutions instead of asking Korima (Raramuri alms), but I saw her hungry and let her go her way.

Traders asked to remove customs and import taxes to compete with their counterparts in El Paso, I think they have the idea that people buy in El Paso solely because of the prices, others asked to remove the Social Security fee, the car lots owners asked for a new decree to pay less for importing cars, others wanted plates for chocolate (illegal) cars, credit words were also requested, expanding SMEs funds, create a free zone, etcetera, etcetera.

The cherry on the cake, straight from "joligud", 15 peasants who went in single file to the back of the room and there with their feet together, holding their hats on with both hands on their chest, and a pout face, listened patiently the exponents until their leader with tears in his eyes asked for help to Secretary of Labor, the bad guys want to get them out of the land they invaded.

And the Cheyenne, 'apa? And the 80,000 bums we have? AY, Barraza! Don't you learn? They're not lazy, they are angels who do not go to school or work because they spend their days at home praying the rosary, and don't come with your ideas of soaping dysfunctional families, single mothers and all that nonsense you write, like video games, when you win, raise the loser's bloody head, well, here it is the same, but cooler, because it's real, you don't understand because you're a retrograde mop.

Of all the "brilliant" speeches, I prefer a phrase someone said and it's attributed to Einstein, which correctly describes this session.

"The stupidity is to believe that there will be different results by doing the same things".

In Memoriam of Carlos Camacho Alcazar

How hard it is to say goodbye to a friend when they leave so unexpectedly. Only a few days ago he would talk proudly to us about the academic achievements of his daughter.

How can we forget his fine humor when he got into waist abusive suppliers?

Carlos Camacho Alcazar, Attorney of PROFECO was kidnapped yesterday at 8:30 when he went down to see what was happening at his neighbors' place.

Carlos was a brave Quixote, a good man always willing to help.

Carlos bravely confronted the U.S. government to prevent the nuclear dump in Sierra Blanca, here, close to Mexico, camping outside the White House, rallies, conferences, letters.

Carlos did everything in his power to stop this dump's construction that would put in serious danger the region. And he achieved it.

As a congressman, he organized society to monitor abuses committed by the customs, in both bridges and in Km. 30 as well.

As the Attorney of PROFECO, he multiplied the action like never before in the city. He was relentless with gas station owners, CFE, Telmex, Cementos Azteca and many others.

Descendant of the founder of the school of Agriculture, Carlos organized frequent meetings with his mother, his brothers and his children. A close family with values that loves the city and has fought for a better place to live.

Today, Carlos Camacho Alcazar is cowardly murdered.

Retaliation against the Federal Government?

Common criminals?

Wrong person?

For an honest man coming from an honest, hardworking family, committed to his city, establishing other lines is an offense.

Rest in Peace, Don Carlos Camacho Alcazar, a hero of our times.

Juarez, the last one out turn off the lights

The wind sweeps the dust and debris from the tiles of the empty parking lot; the signs SALE or RENT decorate the windows of this mall, where a few months ago you could not fit a car in their parking lot.

Mario sold his 3 small business and went south, Ramon is already in El Paso, Jose Enrique was a month out of his business, he was kidnapped, by his return, his employees had already sold all the machinery to get paid for what they were owed. His wife sold the house to rescue him; being 62, he only has his furniture and his wardrobe, his car and truck had to be sold.

Manuel goes to his business secretly, because he fears he is kidnapped again, his debts exceed his assets.

All of them have something in common, they all lost their past, they are as they started, with the aggravating circumstance that they no longer have the strength or youth to start over again, but more serious, they are without hope.

The deputy Cesar Jauregui said in a meeting with a group of journalists that one of the strongest businessmen in Juarez sat at the same table the governor Reyes Baeza with an attorney and the mayor to expose that he was being blackmailed, the governor expressed his regret, to what the dealer said: "the problem, Mr. Governor is that those who collect the cuota are members of the anti-kidnapping committee".

The governor replied quite ceremoniously that they were undercover agents who followed the path of money; "Very smart, Mr. Governor, we've been paying cuotas for 6 months; 26 weeks, how long will it take to track down the money?", the dealer replied.

I understand that we have raised to the altars the "poor people" and the misfortune of "rich people" is joy for some, who can mourn the misfortune of an entrepreneur? They deserve it for glitzy, a PRD troubadour said.

If we have never had respect for working people, we do not understand his tragedy; we can't capture the frustration of someone who loses the assets of a life saved.

We do not understand the vital importance to the economy of a nation that entrepreneurs give, those who have a workshop, a repairing shop, a bakery, a grocery, a factory, a business, because we grew up with stupid Marxist idea of an all-powerful government, we don't realize that the government does not generate a dime, just spend what it collects from those who work.

If we do not protect those who generate wealth, we will sink into the deepest form of poverty.

And, additionally, we have given the tacit consent of the unemployed being able to become a thief, if we do not protect these working men, hordes of thieves will devastate the city to the ground .

In time.

Xenophobia outbreaks in El Paso

WILL Weissert writes in El Paso Times "Ciudad Juarez residents flee Mexico's dying city" http://www.elpasotimes.com/newupdated/ci_16991310

This article gives a description of the events that everyone in Juarez knows and people from El Paso have heard of.

Within the article describes "La Red", a group of Mexican entrepreneurs who have migrated seeking safety in El Paso, this group meets on Thursdays for breakfast and see how they can help each other to succeed in such difficult times after changing their business places.

Changing a business place is not trivial; you have to invest in new facilities, staff training and the heaviest: creating a new market for their products, leaving the previous business in this section of the losses.

The article itself is not aggressive, but when I got to see one of the comments from the readers, I found some incredible pieces of stupidity, ignorance and xenophobia.

Some call to boycott these entrepreneurs, others require them to go south ,but others call them corrupt , money launderers and many more adjectives, which leads me to ask some questions.

Are Mexican entrepreneurs right to go to the United States to place their business?

If we appeal to reciprocity, we only have to see the number of American entrepreneurs who have these in Mexico and around the world. These American companies outside U.S. mainland are so important that without them, the U.S. economy would collapse in days.

Is there corruption in Mexico? Sure there is, the only to remember is that corruption, as we know now it, was invented by American businessmen.

Do Mexicans comply with American entrepreneurs laws? Scrupulously.

Do American companies comply with the laws of different lands? When it is convenient, when it isn't, they skip them, or topple corrupt governments, remember Madero, Salvador, Allende and some more.

Do Mexican businessmen in exile damage El Paso? If you create jobs, generate wealth and contribute to a culture corrupts people, maybe they do.

What does Juarez do for a living? Manufacturing to U.S.

What does El Paso do for a living? Mexicans shopping.

The success of these two cities is a developed symbiosis.

Where are these xenophobic screams coming from? I already said it earlier: stupidity and ignorance of some people and the saddest thing is that despite using pseudonyms in English, by the way they put sentences together, they are "pochos", well, that's how we used to call them in my adolescence to some rim color gringos with a cactus in the forehead, they speak deprecatingly to you for being Mexican and you will still find some of them in schools or migrated.

If both the American people and the Mexican people have been abused by leaders and authorities, wouldn't the time be right to unite and create a community that responds to the interests of society?

To see what unites us beyond outdated nationalism and narrow interests? Mexican businessmen who are migrating are not going to beg or to cause problems, they bring their heritage with risk, they take their creative skills and talents to create wealth. I think they deserve respect, the same we have given in Mexico to American businessmen.

I wish we could keep them in Mexico, or they'll return someday, hopefully, from their self-exile they can assist the land where they were born, there are many ifs on the subject, but I want to highlight one: I wish them well.

My dad is the one who cuts the head off of thugs

Yesterday on the radio program Society and Technology, transmitted from Juarez's station 860 AM, on the subject of "sicarios" and the crucial question was: where were the parents and teachers in the metamorphosis from child to these types of beast as the average age of these animals walk between 16 and 25 years?

There was a call from the audience which told us that last week; the police and the army came to his neighbor's house. They took the little angel out with an arsenal of weapons owned. All the neighbors came out to see what had happened and within minutes the press joined them, a reporter came to the door of the house where a 6 year old was and asked are your dad is?

And the boy replied innocently but very proud: my dad is the one who cuts the head off of "malandros" (thugs). And the listener was wondering what we can expect from this child in the future?

Captain Nunez, who also works as a teacher, commented that a student was driving everyone crazy at his elementary school, so the teachers asked the principal to summon the student's parents to discuss the conduct of the kid.

He tells us that the father came in a leather motorcycle vest with a skull on the back, long dirty hair, a headband, and glassy-eyed bearded, tattooed arms, leather trousers and military boots. In the backseat, the mother was dressed just as the father and drugged to the point of being unable to hold her sight.

"We even had to apologize to them", the Captain finished his comment.

The only thing one can say in these cases is: Long live secular education!

Drug dealers and students united will never be defeated

The student getting shot episode should lead us to several reflections, the first, at first sight, is: it's not possible that a cop shoots a student. Now if we take away their uniforms we have two people, one who walks in fulfilling his work with great stress, knowing that his life is in serious risk, and other marching for a supposed ideal or a cheap grid, however you may want to call it; they meet in the middle of the riot and the crowd begins to insult and stoning federal police, men trained to kill, not to hold mobs, since they didn't bear shields.

This had not happened in Juarez in recent history, so they both have mind only what we see on TV, where the mobs face the police with sticks and these resist the blows with their shields and helmets and sometimes with their bodies, I've never heard anyone saying how they must feel at home when the wounds are healing.

Let's do an exercise; I want you to think for a moment: what would you do if a mob starts insulting you and stone you, would you run? You're not trained to run. Hold? You don't have the gear to hold. Shoot towards the sky? That's what the police did and the insults and stones did not stop, even after shooting one young man, the stones and insults kept going.

I agree that the police should have not shot, but what right do students have to insult and stone the police? Is that the education they are receiving? Those are the ones who will save Juarez? Are robberies, kidnappings and extortions going to end if federal police leave?

It's time to ask rational ideas about the situation, are there are corrupt cops? Yes, there are. Do you see corrupt students? Yes, there are. Are there corrupt teachers? Yes,

53

there are, it seems like the profession is no guarantee of anything anymore, being at cop does not guarantee honesty, same thing with students or teachers, we must analyze the facts coldly, we complain about impunity and students thought that insulting and stoning police would remain unpunished, they thought the police had to endure and be their piñatas, and that was not so.

Today we see a dangerous and exacerbated scenario, the university should keep the flame of freedom burning, but they want to use this flame to burn the city.

Failing War

For generations, after Victoriano Huerta's coup, we started watching how a tyrannical and oppressive system was being built, which canceled the legitimate aspirations of the Mexicans, confiscated their property and desires in favor of men.

The privileged minority monopolized wealth and power, dominating and impoverishing the majority. Those who opposed suffered the fury of power.

Apathy took us to a soft dictatorship where you could only survive, there was an apparent calm like that of the cemetery, the State had control of crime, control and complicity, corruption dominated, but not enough to erase the desires of freedom and democracy of people.

Many were the men who fought against the system with detriment, sometimes even of their life.

In 2000 the Presidency of the Republic was taken from system, but the system remained immovable under legislation that supported it, the owner and master of the system, the PRI maintained within the congress enough soldiers to stop any initiative that tried to go through against the privileges of the status quo.

Fox left Los Pinos as the best manager who this country has ever had, but without being able to change the system. Same thing happens to Calderon, a 3 year term already and the system is almost the same, unions, media, chambers, farmers' organizations, etc. But saying that we haven't progressed would be a huge mistake, today freedom of expression allows us to say and hear things that were previously off limits, the fight against crime has awakened the tiger that swipes everywhere scaring people .

If we compare the current situation with the situation we dream of we are obviously wrong, when compared with other countries, we'll have to see which we are comparing with, when compared to what we were before, now we have a correct diagnosis.

Some people thought that with the triumph of Fox, everything would be magically solved, corrupt people would become honest, trade unions would be free and progressive, society educated and civic, the booming economy and poverty eliminated, and it did not happen. The ballast of tyranny for so many decades couldn't be removed overnight, nor is it free, it's a long and painful process that requires the participation of the whole society, the beast is wounded and attacks everything that moves.

Calderon has taken the bull by the horns and decided to give the fight against organized crime and corruption, no easy task and much less immediate, but wars fatigue and more to a society who became apathetic due to state domination, and this fatigue is paying off the same system, which expects to return to full cart, total domination.

It's hard to know in the morning, when one leaves to work, that he may no longer come back at night, or to his return some hours away someone's missing, but stopping war would be as good as losing it, negotiating would be a great failure and setback.

None of the final strategies have been implemented because the replica changes and the attack must adapt to new circumstances, and those who have the privilege of writing must join this fight because it is a struggle for freedom and well-being. Because we are not spectators, crime offends us, it harms us and whoever fights against it is our ally, if we want all this pain to pay off, we must support the struggle started by Calderon, if we want to return to civil slavery, there's the PRI, waiting for your vote.

The risks of the army in the streets

The arrival of the army to Juarez was received with applause by the people of Juarez; it was strange to see how people opened the window of their cars and reached out to send greetings to the army.

There is an explanation to this behavior in the desire of people to see limited or annulled the action of the drug dealers who lived in a very special pairing with politicians and the Juarez Police Department.

Prove it! Prove it! Outraged politicians would say.

Society has suddenly seen how a carpenter with poor preparation is able to afford a million pesos mansion, his wife drives a brand new luxury car and spends cash, only cash, hand over fist. It's hard to believe that cutting planks in a few weeks you could make that kind of money. we can also see there are places where people go to purchase all kind of illegal drugs and the place remains intact for months and despite regular patrols of the municipal police these places are not closed, then one has to come to the conclusion, either these cops are very clumsy and inept or they are in complicity, and if I may add the intense media reports claiming these facts because the question of evidence?! It is just insulting.

In this framework, the federal police and military "look" the solution, only that there is no substitute for the principles and values and the artificial solution may be worse than the disease.

Today, soldiers are subjected to crime, tomorrow subject to the population?

And it is not alarmist or malicious but they are men; and in every man rests the seed of power in the military, and that is very dangerous. just look at the history of our country, the Mexican Revolution took very few lives, Porfirio resigned as a good Mexican patriot so that no more blood would be shed and so Madero ascended but ambitions from the Generals for power had no limits and blood was shed on the fields with 10% of the population, more than a million people of which the majority were youth.

The military is not trained to the ideological debate or democracy, they are trained to obey and command and its strength lies in weaponry rather than on reason. So we must ask ourselves, what do we want for our country? Blind obedience to a military or diversity of ideas that gives freedom, "sine quam non" for democracy.

NINI pa' cuando

Almost every time when criminals' photos appear in newspapers where we see criminal adolescents, the testimonies of people who have survived kidnappings also report the participation of children and adolescents in the crimes that have terrorized the city.

The most common source of these young offenders is in the group that has graciously been called NINIS; bums who do not go to school or work and devote their energy to leisure, vice and wickedness.

Commentators and most of society tend to justify their activities due to "the lack of opportunities" and grant innocence under their ages, the same laws are generous with them and putting them behind bars is truly impossible.

But the analysis does not stop these criminals, they are advancing day by day in the brutality of the acts without anything to avoid them and the worst, that actually prevents them from doing so, continue to believe that the problems are settled by speeches and diatribes.

We left the ancient model of respect for women as the center of the family, as mentors and caretakers of the children and send them to work to the maquila, the strip clubs or to satisfy the collective lust of irresponsible men, saturating society with bastard children.

Our current brilliant philosophers, with expertise in clay and doctorates in sociology determined that women were equal to men and had the same rights, the moral making them the enslaved servants of man and his children, that women should have the same personal growth as men in the work field, since women were as competent or even more competent and than men. And that women also had the right to sexual freedom that the anachronistic atavism that had convicted them.

The truth is, long story short, it sounds really nice, so nice, that society immediately accepted and assimilated, especially Juarez, where we have not very honorable first place in single mothers and teenage mothers in labor, yesterday I was being told by an officer of SEDESOL the average age of women giving birth was 14 years, a fact that in any developed society would frighten society, but in Juarez we no longer get scared about anything.

Our life is, at this time, in the hands of bastards and I use the term in the full sense of the word, bastards of all ages without any action that can be made to defend ourselves, it is true that the police arrested some and the judicial system lets them back on the street 48 hours later with a triumphant grin that hurts any conscience.

The Governor launches an initiative which is immediately contradicted by the know-it-all sages, but this rhetoric contradictions no viable alternative proposals.

"The army is not a slacker daycare" says an email circulating with the signature of the Colonel, it's true, as is also true that the army lives of the citizens who pay taxes to protect us from "enemies" and if NINIS are potential enemies of society, than this so-called "Colonel's" attitude is what is not justified.

But we as a society have a vital role in this problem. It is time to ask whether we will applaud this relaxation in the way of life carrying a brutal exercise of sex in children and young people, if we will continue pondering as "modern" women deserting from home, if we will continue turning our women into cheap prostitutes, and the crucial question, if we will achieve peace and prosperity in a city besieged by bastards.

Here is the topic on the table, not for reflection or analysis, but to get into the action, either we submit these slackers and put them under control, or they'll end up putting us in the coffin.

If we wanted you dead, you would be dead by now

When we were keeping vigil over Carlos Camacho, delegate from PROFECO in Juarez, a kind, brave and helpful man, we regretted not double checking that it was the army knocking before opening the door. As we were talking here, Carlos saw from his window how the army was coming into his neighborhood, so he went downstairs to see if there was anything that he could do for them, but it turned out they were sicarios and they took him along with other people. The next day, his body was found. He had been beaten to death.

Today, like every other day after finishing the shift at the factory, I did some overtime to check the production reports and prepare the agenda for the next day. Suddenly the doorbell starts ringing insistently. My son goes to answer the door and he returns telling me that there three armed men trying to break inside.

Remembering what happened to Carlos, we didn't let them in so they began banging harder and harder on the door. I started calling all my friends so they would reach the army and verify whether or not they were soldiers, then I dialed the AFI and 060 but nobody would come so these guys would just keep insisting and banging at the door. I called Raul Ruiz, an excellent friend and journalist who was currently on the air on his program, and from there he dialed 060.

From the peephole on my door I told them I was checking their identities and that I would open as soon as I was certain that they were actually soldiers. I asked them to identify themselves and I asked them from which battalion were they but they did not answer me. One of the guys would lift his mask partially from his face to talk and then I started writing down the number of their vehicle so he covered the peephole. With my cell phone I kept talking to my friends and family, even work. An employee who lives across the street said there was a tank pointing to the door.

I explained to the guys on my door what had happened to Carlos Camacho and they simply replied, "if we wanted you dead, you would be dead by now". Such a kind thought from this son of a bitch, now he feels like he owns my life and he has decided to spare my life.

An hour after the first doorbell ring, the AFI arrived and the captain shouted, "We're from the AFI. We're here to protect you. I opened the door for them and about 20 soldiers came into my house. They began to check every single desk and every single drawer in the office. Suddenly, the officer in command from the AFI asks me very angry, "Who opened that hole in the roof? Who escaped from there?" "No one, Sir". I replied. We did it ourselves to get out in case they managed to open the door. I don't have martyr's blood.

The Soldiers got distributed around the floor and all kind of machinery and boxes containing raw material were opened to be checked, and just to be fair they did check everything carefully without damaging anything. the commanding officer or someone who looked like he was in charge came to me and asked me what we did and I said plastic products and machinery upgrading he was interested in the subject so I showed him the machines that were being upgrading. He told me that his son had a very special interest in electronics and while soldiers checked every corner, the commanding officer and I talked about family, production and machines when suddenly a very angry soldier came towards me asking, why did you say we had you kidnapped? I was amazed and told him I never said that.

That's when my new "friend" the commanding officer stood between the both of us and said "let's go. There's nothing here" and they left. 5 minutes later my friends from 860 Radio, from the radio show "Acciones y Reacciones"

(Actions and Reactions) who were calling the authorities throughout all the broadcast and by the end of the broadcast, they immediately came to help me. Cultured and intelligent journalists but overall brave and courageous in the microphone and in a daily basis, thank you very much to them and to my friends who were mobilized immediately, something tells me I owe them a happy ending to this hard incident.

I consider a civil duty to write down this story from a town where no one can feel safe anymore.

Terror in Juarez

Yesterday was a very special day in Juarez. When the executions began in Juarez, life was not substantially affected. Over the months, we learned that a friend's cousin's cousin had been kidnapped or extorted and the morgue would get full of strangers, but soon it would be cousins, neighbors, friends...it was anyone who became subject to violence.

Yesterday we were remembering Carlos Camacho, a delegate from PROFECO, who was kidnapped and killed just a day like yesterday, but on May 17th, 2008. A man who being a political representative went to do a stoppage in the White House In order to prevent a nuclear dump be build in Sierra Blanca, TX. A few kilometers from the border with the state of Chihuahua, the only PAN Representative who opposed the FOBAPROA public debt became an untiring fighter for the highest ideals of a generous and orderly country.

During the day I received several calls, a friend who had to get out of work because their young children had witnessed a murder outside their home and were in shock, a former secretary that was asking me to lend her some money so she could rescue her uncle, a factory worker bursting in tears raising money to bury her son, a friend asking if I knew anyone that would help her accelerate the delivery of the her brother's body from the morgue.

During lunch break, the ambulance sirens could easily be heard, convoys from nervous and frightened police officers, alert at all times with high-powered weapons, at 10 o'clock at night, I left the office, and I found myself with a sight that I had never seen, completely deserted streets, I came across with only 3 cars on the way home.

Enough has been said and written about the origins and blame about violence in Mexico, that President Calderon was the first to challenge them, and that they began to kill each other, they control for the site is being fought for, that it's due to thug returnees, etc. I just want to make a small reflection.

If we take a look throughout world history, we will find that the barbarian and savage tribes became civilizations when they recognized a supreme authority, I won't mention when the concept of God was introduced because the TRIFE won't think twice on giving me a fine, but I invite you to tell me which civilization was built without a God.

Then if a town is subjected to a Divine authority forming a civilization, it is logical to take the concept of society back to barbarism, 200 years leading groups in the dark struggling to eradicate God's name in Mexican society and I think they're finally getting or Do you think that the guys who are beheading and butchering humans have been trained in the fear of God? Today, nobody can accuse us of being polled, backward and illiterate, "semos" very "modernous" and perverts have progressed and this, is the reward for our efforts in this regard.

To covenant or not to covenant?

At the present time, there's a national debate about whether or not the government should negotiate with the crime, some are urging the government to sit down and negotiate with criminals and return the peace, as if we had ever had peace.

Javier Cuellar expressed surprise by my article NO! Mr. Sicilia. NO! , Which expose the position NOT to negotiate with crime by the state and it would be enough to remind the mission of any State to surprised Mr. Cuellar, and understanding that in a state – crime covenant, society is the most affected.

In this article I present the testimony of Mariano José de Larra, who lived in Morelos, and lived the PEACE that Cuellar is asking for. Where bullets were shot in one direction. Heading from crime to society. Where complaints were drowned in the closest circle to the victim, where red top journalism doesn't exist because nobody ever gets caught and complainants ended up being accused by the state thanks to this joke called covenant and the State – Crime association.

Mr. Cuellar, you call me naive because you intend an antagonistic state towards crime. I like the adjective because my naivety is based on hope, however, you are also naïve to claim that a deal would end the kidnappings, robberies and extortion, not only your ingenuity is born from hope, but of ignorance as well. And I will continue with my nonsense, as you call it Mr. Cuellar. Do you think that when the government decides to covenant up with the criminals, kidnappers who make a fortune in one kidnapping will go back to work at the maquila for 700 pesos a week? Stating that, I'm not laughing very much.

Opinion is divided among spokesmen and I think that I prefer to dance to transparency and the rule of law that the opacity and crime, we dance in different opinions my dear Cuellar.

Ties up his speech by saying, "so then, we can only covenant and both sides have always had excellent negotiators so don't worry about it" I understand that Dionisio is who you dance to.

Fallibility is inherent in human beings and thus to society, thinking about the perfect society is a utopia but we must guide the helm in that direction, as the simplistic solutions proposed will only give us a terrible result. We have lived through this before; it's neither an easy task nor a single person task. It's something that can only succeed with the support of the whole society.

We are facing a silent majority who lives from their work, is looking for happiness, peace and harmonious coexistence. On the other hand, there's a violent, rich and powerful minority that seizes the assets of those who work, who profit health and wellness of the majority. Which side should the state be in? Which side are you, Mr. Cuellar?

NO! Mr. Sicilia. NO!

A pamphlet entitled "¡Estamos hasta la madre!" (We've had enough!) is going viral on the internet. Written by Javier Sicilia where, among other things, it demands the federal government to covenant with crime.

What would actually happen with a covenant isn't necessary to imagine, living in the area where his son was killed has been done and I will quote Mariano de Larra's research that lives in that area, to describe what would happen with a covenant.

"The hostages were many thousands (a single family kidnapped 3000), the number of deceased could never be told, because everything happened at the worst and most sinister arrogance and in secrecy. The bodies of the kidnapped and murdered inhabit the hillside of the federal highways. First, the hostages were kept in the town of Huitzilac and then the cells of the State Attorney.

Evil, impunity and cynicism became so serious that when the hostages had paid what they demanded, they were still kept in the same holding cells of the Attorney General, but now as kidnappers.

The governor, the mayor and the police chief of Morelos were, all, drug dealers, extortionists, kidnappers and murderers."

We set the example of Morelos because that's where the murder of Sicilia's son occurred, but the entire country was immersed in the same excesses.

But only one side killed, the murderers related with the Cartels who had power and nothing but power, only one side died, from ordinary citizens THOSE WHO NOBODY, ABSOLUTELY NOBODY, WOULD DEFEND, and, apparently, and in retrospect we defend, because now we claim as wise men   these monsters who murdered and annoyed to the point of nausea.

Mr. Sicilia, we are also ¡hasta la madre!

We've had enough about the government claiming that the state's fight against crime is responsible for all this violence. It is the sole responsibility of offenders.

We've had enough of being told that we must return to the   dealings   with   criminals. Is all that junk that has brought us here and who want to return to it will have to deal with each of those we do not agree. We should also be taken into account.

But in the event that this requirement is catered would ask Mr. Sicilia: how would this covenant with the criminals work? Would there be a round-table including authorities as well as with criminals in order to give the plazas to the highest bidder... I the authority asking the narcos: Who wants to poison the north of the country? Or by turns: Who wants to poison elementary school children, who wants the middle school, who wants those from high school and college, who wants the general public? How much do you offer for the line of   business? Then, in behalf of the kidnappers, how much will we receive from each hostage getting rescued? Who will murder those who do not pay? Do we just kidnap and you play pretend as if you cared?

Tell me Mr. Sicilia: How would that state - crime covenant work? And I ask because your magazine "Proceso", invested in a costume martyr, has been accused of dealing with criminals who sell them to appear or not appear in your magazine.

How do you negotiate your articles? It is true that we've had enough, leaving every day to work with the anxiety that we might get carjacked at gun point, that we might get kidnapped, extorted, robbed, or even running into the streets with decapitated bodies, open any newspaper and watch how blood gets spilled.

It is true that we've had enough of waiting anxiously for our relatives when they get even a little delayed or they're without communication for any reason, but from this point to giving up in the fight against crime is a huge difference.

Perhaps for a narco journalist, as you seem to be, that is a great start and a great business, but for the vast majority of Mexicans, without influence, without microphones, without hope, the great ideal should be living in a country crime-free instead of a place of peace and mutual responsibility.

The fight against crime should be everyone's task that starts at home with the education of our children, extending to work, school, the neighborhood, which at every point wherever we are, let's be promoters of honesty, integrity, respect, in few words, of all the values that lead to have a peaceful and productive society.

Covenants with crime NEVER! Mr. Sicilia.

Impunity

A few weeks ago I was publishing an article which I named "legality or justice" in which that gap that has formed between legality and justice was strongly stressed; between what we expect of authority and what we get from it, one of the conclusions that stood was "the law promotes injustice and promotes impunity".
A few days after writing this, life gave me a chance to document it step by step -and I say life because if, by any reason I say God, the TRIFE won't think twice to come give me a fine-, you can see the obsession of the system by having an atheist society.

We were finishing a meeting, when we turn on the cell phones a friend gets a call to to let him know that they had caught a couple of thugs robbing his business and that they were taken by police officers who were heading to the Aldama station. So, my friend had to go to there, take the minutes a couple of minutes and make a report.

I offered to go with him and we arrived to the station in a few minutes. We were sent to a room where the police officers were describing what happened. Another officer was writing the report... and you could see both thugs completely drugged and the employee giving his testimony.

During the weekend, some thieves had broken into and they had looted everything they could, including air conditioners and heaters. By Monday, when the clerk arrived, he was amazed to see the door open. As soon as he went in, he heard a loud bang and he saw a pair of guys hitting and destroying sheetrock walls to steal the metal frames. He immediately got to a safe distance where he called the police, but as the minutes passed and the police did not arrive he decided to insist and kept calling. After one hour and five calls, police finally arrived and caught the thugs.

We spend three hours at court sitting about 5 feet away from the thugs but face to face, halfway through a policeman came and joked with thugs, then came human rights and asked if they had been treated well in the arrest and answered "YES" but then abounded and asked if anything hurt, which they immediately decided to put their acting skills to the test and put some sort of hurt puppy face, and the thugs replied that their arms ached, just from where they were seized. "anything else?" the lawyers insisted, our back hurt, the thugs responded with the same puppy face, so the human rights lawyers took some notes and left. Passing in front of us they looked at us disapprovingly and kept their way, standing tall as if they were some kind of heroes.

They took us out of this room and they asked us to wait in the reception, where we would be told when to go to the "Averiguaciones Previas" Department. We spent an hour waiting and nothing happened, so we decided to approached and ask and we were sent to "previas". By the time we got there, we could not get in because we were tackled by the Family of one of the prisoners. "They're innocent!" The family would shout. "You're making a mistake". And they would show us a baby while asking us, "Who will look after him now? Look at him, this poor, sick child, the employee retreated and that's when others came to intimidate him and to say they had seen that he was the thief, that they could identify him and his truck, and that this was not going to stay like this. They were going to find a way to get even at him.

After over an hour we made our way and arrived at the offices of ministerial agents, there, the mother of the other prisoner was waiting for us. who, for some reason, was not threatening, but instead she pleaded us not to press charges since she was a single mother and had to work to support her 3 children, we tried to locate an agent but it would take more than an hour to accommodate us, so between her threats and pleadings the complaint by the employee first filed and then while my friend made his declaration his employee came back really frightened. Outside, the rest of the gang was waiting for him and they wanted to take him, "Aren't you going to do anything?" We asked the agents, "raise your complaint for threats" the agent replied harshly. "Oh, should I file it before or after getting killed?" I asked astonished, I did not get an answer this time. So I took the employee and by the back door we got to the parking lot and decided to stay hidden in the back of my car while my friend finished his declaration. It must have been well past 10p.m. when we left "previas", 10 exact hours of paperwork with the task of taking the next day, the deed to the property, invoices for everything that had been stolen and the possibly even my great-grandmother's marriage certificate.

The next day we went to the maquila where one of the "moms" works. She had repeatedly been calling my friend on his cell phone; the authorities had the liberty to give the thugs all the personal information of their accusers. Later that day, we took the missing papers, during the afternoon we received a phone call because one of the scripts was missing a seal and the invoices needed to be, original and signed by the accountant or two witnesses, but the worst thing was that the employee had failed to recognize the thugs and we had lost the case because of that.

We ask the coordinator to explain how it that the employee had not recognized the thieves was. "We showed him 5 pictures and he said that the ones he recognized were not the thugs". "Hold on" I said, "Show me the pictures". And there they were. 5 pictures from a paper printer. 5 bond paper in black in white. 5 thugs, that thanks to the quality of those pictures, they would almost look the same. Not even their mothers would recognize them one from another.

Now I asked.

-But you caught them in flagrante! what is the purpose of this recognition?

-The law is the law, he replied solemnly as if the heavens had opened to light him and make him shine with majestic glory.

-I see! Well, it seems we have such smart legislators, and even smarter those who seem to interpret how laws work, I intervened in the conversation, the coordinator smiled... by the things work here, it seems she had failed guessing my sarcasm.

So I continued in that solemn tone on my speech.

- "The only thing left is for you to make an agreement so they can repair the damage." the coordinator said.

-"They don't work or study. How will they get money to pay me? Will they go and murder, kidnap or rob someone in order to pay me? Aren't you worried that these guys will go and kill one of your family members for a few pesos?" My friend asked.

-"The law is the law, we must make an agreement." The coordinator insisted.

'Well give me time to think, replied my friend.

An hour later we returned to the coordinator,

I already have the idea of the agreement, getting two guys out of their criminal lives. Number one in the agreement, have them stop doing drugs and have them submit an anti-doping every week. Number two, have them go back to school and show proof of their attendance with the anti-doping. Number three, have them work from home. Number four, have them do community service.

They brought the crooks in so they could speak with him and he talked for about two hours with offenders. They talked about the possibility of getting back on tracks taking advantage of the agreement, maybe going into re-hab. Afterwards, the mothers came in and again a long talk about the need to support their children in the agreement. The day ended and we were asked to come back the next day first

74

thing in the morning. At noon, the 48 hours period would expire and they had to set them free if things were not fixed.

We arrived early and the employee started working on settling the general agreement. Halfway through, the crooks' lawyer embraced the crooks and their mothers. It was all laughter and joy. One of the mothers signed a promissory note to him, the other one gave him a bag with something which he immediately tried to hide in his pocket. An hour later, he received the agreement so he could read it. -"Very well then, the boys will sweep the floor in front of your business once a week for six months. This will do as a repairing for the damage caused and community service as well".

My friend was shocked and told the bureaucrat, -"This is not what we agreed to." -"What you want is against the rights of boys." Which he also replied with solemnity that quickly spread all over the room.

-"If you don't write down what we agreed, I'm not signing that paper." My friend stated emphatically. -"You are one obtuse and stubborn man." the bureaucrat told my friend in a derogatory way. - Obtuse your "# $% & / mother. My friend replied indignantly.

And the insult exchange began… the shouting, the crying mothers, the frayed boys and by the time that the beatings were about to start, two guys came in and took away my friend.

On his way out, a lawyer in his late years came and said, "Don't waste your time or risk your lives. The judiciary is fully infiltrated. The system is poisoned."

We went out through the back door. And as Dostoevsky would say, Insulted and Injured. It seems that I didn't read this story nor was it told to me. I experienced it myself, front row tickets. I know that nothing is going to change, we are a coward and frightened society that can be stepped on by the system's will, but I think it is my citizen duty to give testimony about these events.

(Last minute update) Yesterday with a pick-up truck, the gate to the parking lot entrance was knocked down and it seems that they broke inside again. My friend called me and asked should he do this time. I just replied, "Fix the door, my friend. We're in a country where the law has already killed justice."

The ones who left

When my friends from other cities ask me what am I still doing in Juarez, I say, "like the poet of the people. And with every day that goes by, I find another reason to leave, but everyday a feeling springs out of me to stay and here I am, I find myself stunned between the feelings of fear and hope.

Last week I listened attentively details of the kidnapping of a friend, twenty days when his temples turned gray; he lost his heritage and most serious, he lost peace, serenity, and self-assurance. I saw his face and found new wrinkles on his face, I felt his pain as if it were my mine because it reminded me of own pain.

I remember the afternoon that three masked men were beating at my door demanding me to let them in; the phone calls to the police who never came, the paraphernalia feeling vulnerable, the rage of impotence just two weeks after we buried Carlos, who was murdered in very similar circumstances.

Last Friday I was walking in Mesa St. at El Paso, TX, and it was curious seeing how many cars were parked outside bars and restaurants, the bustle of a city used to be calm and quiet, was now filled with giggles and joy of what has been called "The New Juarez". Crossing the bridge back to Juarez, every light of every clubs was off. It had been less than two years when these streets teemed with people. Now, just empty streets and lifeless windows.

Doctors have been on strike and have begun asking for more security, and their requests are very fair, as fair as useless, we do not realize the depth of the problem, we would have to assume a gigantic responsibility in this pandemonium.

As children we were taught that the rich are evil and the good poor; that entrepreneurs are wicked exploiters and workers suffered poor things; that the poor exist because someone stayed with their money and that someone is the evil rich.

In high school there's always a teacher who opens our eyes to tell us that the bourgeoisie must die, that the only solution is the dictatorship of the proletariat.

Politicians in campaign and many of those already installed in power in every speech they summon the "50 million Mexicans who are living in extreme poverty," and assure us that they will be fighting for these poor. We have been brainwashed again and again, over one hundred years with this same speech and the poor are still poor, the rich are still rich and redemption fails.

Well then, if the government has not given them the money that was promised, some have already decided to take it. But ... Who is poor? And who is rich? Starting from scratch, you could say that the poor are the one living in remote colonies and the rich are the ones living in the best neighborhoods. But it's not exactly this way, because the moment of seeing the kidnapping of the owner of a small grocery store, a taqueria, a workshop, an engineer, an architect or a doctor we realize that anyone can be considered rich and anyone can feel poor.

We have been trained in the ideology of class struggle, the ideology of the thief and assassin, in the cult of social sicarios, in the retrograde and bestial Marxism, and still dare to ask ourselves "what's going on?"

We are reaping what we sow for years, left the path of virtue by perversion, we pulled over the doctrine of work for social revenge, and we took out the priests from schools at gunpoint and installed the rational education. We decided to exchange Values for consciousness.

I fully understand the ones who left, but I admire those who have stayed, and those who continue risking their lives every day; the ones who haven't dropped the towel and believe that this city still has a cure. The ones who still have hope and are still praying for this city. This city generated vast utilities and salaries above the national average, we enjoyed better roads than in most of the country, there was plenty of work and entertainment in abundance, and we enjoyed a magnificent sky.

This was a land of great leads, where are they? Are they at Starbucks in down in Mesa Street?

The city generated powerful and wealthy businessmen. Is Red Lobster in their place now? They say that women from Chihuahua are brave, because when her men were working in the mine, they would defend their people from the Apaches. Do you think such women still exist?

Many are safe in El Paso and I don't criticize them, as Nietzsche would say "Human, All Too Human", but sometimes the temptation to create imaginary scenarios arises. Let's say, what if the ones who left came back with all their talent, all their strength and all their money to get the city back for the good people?, If they would give a decisive battle against crime? If every juarense would take a gun and we cleared citizenship? What if we joined the struggle of all the doctors?

Yes, I know, is a utopia. Solidarity is not part of our education, marital value is not in our case, but sometimes we like to dream in order to forget our nightmares.

Alleged suspect

When microprocessors became more powerful the abandonment of the old mainframes became evident by many users which change their old machines with new ones based on this technology.

This change had some major challenges. While the traditional language to attract new machines was relatively easy, it was necessary to recompile programs and data which could capture them again, making this, a mammoth task in different levels.

As every crisis creates an opportunity, we took on the task of making a device that could connect the two types of machine and made programs that would allow the making of modifications, we were soon saturated with customers.

The presidency of the republic, in times of Zedillo, had a Cyberg that had not been disposed of due to the information that it contained, we were called to make the change, a task that took us almost 6 months, I'm just writing all this as a preamble to the main topic.

It seemed very funny how all officials close to the president spoke the same way as he did, stood the same way as he did and adopted the same positions as President Zedillo, so we referred to them as "presidentitos", but spending time with them every day took me to see that it was something natural, Salinas officials also spoke in the tone of his former boss and what about those who worked with Echeverría despite many years, they continued having that peculiar tone.

A psychologist was explaining to me that the imitation phenomenon occurs with people around the leader or the boss, and that it goes beyond the talking. Imitating reaches behavior and attitudes as well.

In Juarez have a leader that comes out bragging that he just got out of his Kickboxing class, that challenges the federal police, someone who walks around with armed groups in unmarked vehicles without uniforms that look more like sicarios than bodyguards, a business leader who feels as if he owns the city and doesn't mind to say it out loud, as when he was arrested by the federal police.

A ruling style closer the dictatorship than to an actual democracy, vested with authority bordering on arrogance and authoritarian rule, but the "tetitos" (Little tetos) are a much more dangerous imitation than the leader. And if this seems like a joke right now, his rivals fall into an even more pathetic level.

These so-called authorities have developed a trend for ambushing people who have the need to leave their work during night shifts, and even when citizens prove that they are hard working people, sometimes they are arrested for no reason. However, they're given a chance to "arreglarse", which is, to come to an informal agreement in order not to be taken to jail. After all, their boss needs a lot of money for his next political campaign. And there go the less fortunate citizens, up and down in a police car until their relatives gather enough money to set them free.

This is not new news, this has even been on foreign TV shows, but it seems that here we have learned to tolerate villains who dress up as officers all because we live in fear of reprisals, we have learned to no longer questioning violent officials. That civic courage that 25 years ago put us as an example to the world sold out seems to have faded away and today we are a frightened and gagged society, we only have enough courage to criticize President Calderon, since nobody actually steps up for him, but just looking at "teto" in a wrong way can be a very delicate matter.

I'm not talking to you about something I heard or someone told me, I kept a case step –by – step, and I want to say that we are alone, we have no defense against thugs or against municipal, as my grandparents would day, "Let God have mercy on Juarez".

Juarez… Narco - society?

In the last debate that was carried out among the contenders for mayor of Juarez, something unusual happened, César Jáuregui candidate for the PAN presented a forceful argument to present evidence of drug trafficking activities of former Juarez Mayor Hector "Teto" Murguia, now as a candidate again for mayor; in addition, evidence of inexplicable wealth was also shown. However, the narco-politician didn't even get upset. "Look, Cesarín" answered while the audience bursts out laughing, "I got all that and even more. You will never dream even with what I have on my property declaration".

This, in a civilized city, would have been a scandal of major proportions, but not in Juarez, the media only reported that Cesar Jáuregui had lowered the level of the debate; no commentator noted how serious it was that a narco could be elected for mayor. In a city where narcos kill each other every day, where companies are extorted and entrepreneurs kidnapped, where thousands end their early lives by excessive drugs use or jump to criminal lives to get some cash for a piece of junk car or an illegal dose.

Here, nothing really happened, "that damned Jáuregui. It's not like if he told us something that we didn't know," some said. "It's a dirty war" the know-it-all townies would say, "better the devil you than the one you don't" others said that the elections were given away to teto, with all his crimes, theft, corruption and whatever build up this week. he "clearly" won. And soon, his Majesty Teto I, ruler of the throne of Juarez will ascend and people will applaud, the media will run to give every meaningless detail, "Armando, here comes Teto just leaving his home, and blah, blah, blah" a reporter said excitedly as if narrating the departure of Queen Elizabeth and Prince Antonio.

Perhaps Kafka could explain this cult to crime, to the dark side, and if you are heading towards the slums, you'll be able to listen to house stereos listening to loud music, especially Narcocorridos and now, Sicario-corridos, some supporters of the PAN speak of the transports, of vote buying, power among narcos being shared, large amount of money spilled among political leaders and media, but reality is that if people had actually come out to vote, if people had actually cared, teto wouldn't have won.

How to explain this absence, this passive complicity of the population? The drug dealing and narco is not new in Juarez, drug dealers were established decades ago and people knew of their activities. Believe it or not, they were accepted, the ladies used to go to the best clubs, the children attended the best schools, vendors approached them, architects, engineers, joiners you fought the build its lavish homes, they were asked for loans to solve personal problems, and even one served as judge in disputes and came to his arbitration when they began.

"The narco has always existed and it will keep on existing", a political commentator once said, and he began to give dates and places where drugs are sold and nothing ever happened. Because the narco has financed political campaigns, placed and removed rulers at all levels, the PRI was the great narco administrator and nothing ever happened. They knew, everybody knew, but, what could be done? "This is the way things are", the resigned would say.

Until one day someone thought a drug war had to be done. And soon, interests in many different levels of society started falling apart; "things will get fixed soon" the political sages would say at the beginning of the hostilities; "Calderon should have prepared before embarking on this new adventure" others would say; "Calderon must negotiate" said others; "Calderon is to blame for everything" the media said.

Now it seems that those who want to eliminate the problem are the ones to blame for the existence of the problem, "shoot the messenger" the King said whenever he received any kind of bad news.

This gives us a level of how it was that society started corrupting without realizing it, that this level is as a group and that the real question is... is Juarez a narco - society?, Many will think that it actually is.

Everything is President Calderón's fault

- Vieja, it's too hot!!
- Yeah, it's Calderón's fault!!
- My friend, the flu got me really hard this time.
- Sure thing buddy, I'm sure it was Felipe Calderón's fault.
- Damn it! I lost the spare tire.
- It must have been the Feds.

Here in Juarez, every bad thing that happens is either Felipe Calderón's fault or the Federal government's fault. Our brainy radio talk, newspapers and television are all attribute it to President Calderón.

Before Calderon became president, Chihuahua was a paradise, but since Calderón became president everything is upside down, or at least that's what the juareños "journalists" like to say. Just to let you know, every day there is a radio program at noon that lasts two hours, where two monkeys named Gomez pretend to be broadcasters and they like to link all the bad news with Calderon and his government. That constant gallop without answer only causes distorts and a collective unconscious, creating a hatred towards our President and hiding the reality of the problems and their makers.

Chihuahua has been ruled only for 6 years by the opposition and all its evils come from Calderon.

In a local broadcaster there was a memorandum that read "those who use the microphones established in these radio station to attack the Mayor or the Governor, these doors will be closed. Against the President of the Republic, feel free to say whatever you like". That was the editorial line of the radio, but if we see the contents of the others, on channel 44 and the Diario de Juárez, it's just the same. The PRI is sanctified and Calderon gets a beating.

This process of publicly lynching the Shorty distorts the nature of the problem and hides the real culprits of the violence in Juarez. No media emphasizes the seriousness of the existence of these monsters that roam the city killing, stealing, extortion and kidnapping.

Nobody speaks about those who have been benefited from the sale and trafficking of drugs, nobody listens of the great mansions of the traffickers or their "parallel" activities.

"We can get killed for those stories" a journalist friend used to tell me. "You don't know what it's like being forced to say certain things".

Mmmm interesting, we must attack hard, but only Calderon, and impute him all the problems because there will be no retaliation, such courageous of journalists! Although many deprived people talking about the illegal activities of the state and municipal authorities, journalists do not dare to open their mouths and are forced to attack the president, and even more, with the PRI at command, like I always say, "el chayote es el chayote".

I police, you police, the police, BINGO!

I think it's a midway point between tragic and comic to hear our politicians swollen chest facing the sky and shouting with some sort of hero accent, "The primary obligation of the state is to ensure the safety of citizens" and then talk radio, television and newspapers as if they were parrots repeating the same words again and again.

Well I have a new bad news that does not exist in the Constitution, the state does not mark any obligation to its subjects, with the recent reforms something was changed on the subject of security, the text is now: "Public safety is a function by the Federation, the Federal District, states and municipalities, include prevention of crime, the investigation and prosecution to make it effective."

The design of the Constitution was not meant to protect the public or give the people guarantees or rights, it was made to control and exploit the people, every president has done the reforms wanted to adapt it to their particular way of governing, to keep their absolute master status for 6 years.

The issue of public safety has been elevated to constitutional status, which by the way is another joke from our politicians, when you want to emphasize a law elevate the constitutional anyone been told that the Constitution of a country is the letter described as being made the country not a compendium of laws. So we have very advanced constitutions that are no longer than 10 pagers, the Constitution from the U.S. fits into a poster, and we have an obtuse 170 pages grimoire full of contradictions, poorly structured that sometimes wants to be a law, other prison rules, another good intentions, some letters to Santa Claus etc... I always thought that it was probably written by Cantinflas.

Now the Constitution includes "the three orders of government must coordinate with each other to meet the goals of public safety" in Juarez this has been interpreted as: "You shoot me, he shoots me, who shot me?"

All this comes as a prelude to the case of the federal police who confronted escort the mayor of Juarez better known as Teto.

Teto became the spokesperson for his escort without even having witnessed the events he gave a detailed and emphatic version to the media, and then emerged as judge and executioner calling for the immediate retreat of federal officers in Juarez, which would be his kingdom for the next 3 years, "Gentlemen, out of my business." There were some timid statements from the federal officers which didn't have the same impact nor were they emphasizes, spreading the version where they claimed that the mayor did not stop when they asked him to stop his escort, but they were able to see that they had high powered weapons.

Which version should we believe?

The one that has been widely disseminated or logic?

To find the logic would have to ask several questions:

Is Teto's escort arrogant?

Is Teto arrogant?

During the campaign, Teto promised to kick out the federal police from Juarez.

Was that promise left out afterwards, or was the population necessary for the activities of Teto?

Now we make some remarks with federal, we are continually hearing reports of clashes between sicarios and federal reporting them they're armed men in one direction, they come and there is an exchange of gunfire in which a bodyguard dies, in a land where the lie is political art hardly know who is telling the truth, but back to the Constitution and ask:

Are they coordinating as the Constitution requires?

Were the escorts police or civilians?

Are the vans they were traveling escorts wore ID?

Do you think the federal officers had shot municipal officers aboard police patrols?

And one last question:

Who should leave the city, the Feds or Teto?

You will have the best conclusion, I have mine and it's not the most popular.

They do know how to negotiate

Last night I was woken up by gunfire, then the second one I heard it while I was wide awake, and if there was a third one I didn't realize it because I had already fallen asleep again, but then came the ambulances and police with sirens as loud as possible. I don't understand, why won't they turn off the sirens if they're parked? So I had to get up to close the window and cover my ears with the pillow to sleep again.

"Oh, Calderon... sigh..." how did he ever come up with this idea of a war against crime? But, guess what? Now that the PRI won the elections again, the war is over and peace shall return. Well, we all know it's nothing but words, but that's what the "candidote", the PRI governor and his gang say... gang? Sorry, I meant campaign.

Since lately I've been a little slower than average and I'm not really catching ideas clearly, I would like you to help me understand this about negotiating with the narco. I imagine sitting in front of a large conference table and a large map will be displayed and the areas, better known as plazas, will be divided.

And of course, they will take a market study to help them negotiate and I imagine that the future governor will say, "Let's see, in this area there are 100,000 addicts who consume 2 doses per day for 100 pesos which gives 20 million pesos per day. The starting bid is $9 million a day, who's the highest bidder?

I imagine that the thugs will make some gesture of disapproval and say, "That's a lot of money. We have expenses, distribution, collection you know it. We might get caught by soldiers and they'll take the cargo.

-"Hold on a second", the governor interrupted. Why do you think we have police cars?

- They distribute and collect, you deliver us the cargo and you'll get your share, and viola! Just make sure that you dedicate yourself to people, we do the rest. What else will these guys talk about in the negotiation? Will it be in dollars or pesos? Will cash get a discount? Maybe cash down for the initial purchase? Will there be any laboratories to inspect the quality?

Or maybe the negotiation will take place not by areas, but as a whole business line? Let's see, who wants to spoil and mess to school sector? Who wants the clubs? Who would like to have the picaderos? How much for the street?

How would you they negotiate? I ask because in all of their campaign speeches, they have never given details about anything. However, when they are questioned by their own people they get very upset and in a very authoritarian way they start preaching on how narco has always existed... just as prostitution is a necessary evil, we must accept them, but have them controlled.

Also robberies, murders, rapes etc, have always existed. How are we to negotiate with them? "Let's see, you kill, we catch you, you give us some cash, we let go... you steal, you share, if you get caught, you give the judge some cash and he lets you go.

Well that is just awesome! The PRI has been right all along. Everything has always existed. In that case, everything is negotiable! The PRI are geniuses. Now I understand the full car and their eighty years of absolute power. Well, let's erase the last 10 years as presidents from President Fox and President Calderón, but not to worry, there are still many state Governors and city Mayors that hold up high the banner for the PRI, now we just have to hold on for a little more than two years and superboy will restore peace and order. Long live the PRI, Sir, yes, Sir! Back to negotiating with narcos, extortionists, kidnappers, thieves, murderers, rapists, etcetera... Count me in boys, I will vote for the PRI, so peace is restored... oh! Just don't forget my 200 pesos, my sandwich and my "pecsi" Viva Mexico!

Todos Somos Juarez

I read an article that appeared in the Newspaper El Universal Venezuela about the failure of the program Todos Somos Juarez, and I thought on researching this program. I called a friend to see if he knew anyone in this program and I got the phone number of Humberto Uranga. I called him and made an appointment for an interview.

I arrived a little late to our appointment so I was greeted with a joke about my punctuality. It's customary to address people according to their academic background Here in Mexico, so I asked,

-"Licenciado or Ingeniero… How should I address you?"

- "Citizen" he replied. "Damn it" I thought. I've never interviewed a citizen so I asked, -"Can I call you Humberto?", -"Of course." He replied. So I started the interview.

-"Do you think that all of us are Juarez?"

-"No, but we could be." he said emphatically while still looking at his computer's monitor. - "And this program, will make us feel that all of us are Juarez?" I asked with a grin.

- "We won't know unless we try." He replied with a scathing behavior.

- "What are you looking for with this program?"

- "Regain security rates and restore the quality of life." He answered.

- My next question was if this program had been a failure. But I thought to myself that the question is meaningless since the results are obvious. After the program, now we have more violence and less quality of life.

-"Your perspective is unclear. Violence is not generated by the program, but the solution may actually be found in this program". The official replied.

- Any crystal wand? I asked.

He took a piece of paper and he started drawing a stool with 3 legs, 3 legs that were on the same side. If you give the sketch of this outline to a carpenter for him to build it, it will surely keep falling all day long.

One leg represents the participation of all; the following represents mutual responsibility and the last one represents integrity. To be honest, I didn't understand either, so I asked in a way that he wouldn't notice my ignorance,

-"How have you decided to develop each leg?"

-"We have formed an analysis of the problem and its solution table with the community, organized groups have participated and now we have channeled $27 million pesos for 40 NGOs in integrity, we are repairing the urban infrastructure to serve as a self-sustaining society we have renovated public parks, hospitals, auditoriums, nurseries... in few words, everything that helps the quality of life of the citizens."

-Interesting, but I think you skipped mutual responsibility.

- It is something that we're barely working on. During the government of Baeza, we couldn't get the governor to participate. Every time we tried to talk about security, he would simply look the other way. He was not involved. However, Cesar Duarte, the current governed seems to be compromised. As a short example, during Baeza's government, from every 100 caught criminals, 98 were released. Today, the numbers are reversed, from every 100 caught criminals, 98 are held. During the previous government, allegations phones, security cameras, everything was in the wrong hands.

When it comes to the police, it's a very serious problem. We made a complaint against some federal police and internal affairs removed them immediately. But in state and municipal police there is nothing that can be done. The answer to any attempt is that people cannot be removed from their positions or relocated, period! The level of infiltration of corrupted forces is remarkable. We're working on mined land, the size of the monster is disproportionate, if the debugging process of the state and municipal police ever ends it would be glimpsing... it would be the beginning of the end, but the good news is that now there will be coordination between state and federation.

-"Will the program continue this year?"

- "Well, of course. We have a budget of one billion to support Juarez's society.

-"Humberto, One last question, do you believe in this project?"

Yes, definitely, I believe in the program, I believe in my people and I think we will overcome this crisis together.

-"Humberto, I really appreciate your words and your attention."

Juarez, heading where?

In "The End of Eternity" by Isaac Asimov, the author states time traveling as no one had done, laying the groundwork for the books and films that have been made on this subject. On it, the executor, Harlan, time-travels to make minimal changes to correct wars or catastrophes.

And history is made of small changes that cause large movements. During the eighties, a change in Juarez would generate large movements that would quickly spread across the whole country; the people of Juarez defeated the system.

This epic moment is not publicly remembered, and it seems that nobody wants to know about it. A civil society movement defeated the Mexican predator system and kept it off for almost 20 years in which the change was more than obvious. a city whose whorehouses on Juarez Street used to be the main attraction became the city with the best industrial infrastructure in Mexico, broad avenues and incredible economic growth, jobs, training of qualified personnel in manufacturing and all that entails .

But the system did not fail to operate, the corrupted and the media did underground work to discredit what had been done and the so-called "heroes" believed them, creating an internal struggle that led them to lose power, but worst of all, that it led them to lose their authority.

The system was lurking and in 2004 it returned with all the fury contained in "Teto".

Everything that people believed was in the past rose again, with the aggravating circumstance of having no real opposition while the PAN members were at home ruminating their internal struggles, their disappointments and their tantrums.

Rivers of public funds focused toward the media, no potholes were covered in the streets consciences were silenced, corrective corruption returned, not that I mean that the PAN administrations were immaculate, but the war cry of "there's enough for everybody" arose as a battle flag, the "jackpot" gathered by innocent people returned thanks to the police and transit, fees the contractor and suppliers, 15% for Teto, the picaderos tripled and police cars were used to "distribute and collect". Teto dominated everything and became rich as if money was falling from the sky. However, he never forgot the "progresitos" who he embraced so they could be in the picture together just by feeding them some crumbs they were dragged to his feet, he began to command gangs and he gave them an unusual power, turning him into the big boss.

The media were silent, Who complains while having a full stomach?, As said a post-it in the cab of a broadcaster "those who use the microphones established in these radio station to attack the Mayor or the Governor, these doors will be closed. Against the Federal government or the President of the Republic, feel free to say whatever you like. Calderon is to blame for everything and careful who says otherwise."

Today, Teto returns with a bulging wallet spreading and spending money everywhere, "he DOES know how to rule"… and it's true , if ruling is, similar to dominate, to loot, to corrupt , in few words, everything that the system has been doing since the coup d'état in 1913.

This 4th of July we do change the future by depositing our vote. It won't be the wonderful change that we expect; nor will fairy godmothers from Sleeping Beauty come to transform everything with their magic wand. It's just leaving a predatory beast roadside and to keep fighting to rebuild the city where we live.

Has the violence in Juarez left us any lesson?

When one studies the history of mankind, we easily falls into the temptation to study only the greatness of the works that were left us, but rarely in the methodology that led them to acquire those skills that amaze us.

A notable case is the Mayan culture, their calendars had a very careful record of both natural phenomena such as social and repeating certain events helped them establish astronomical and agricultural cycles. In the social aspect, the analysis of the facts was taken into account to determine which behaviors were good, healthy, and positive; this knowledge made their laws and regulations.

And if you don't want to go as far back as the Mayan times or the Egyptians, in the villages it was very common that at dusk ladies in their neighborhood would sit down and "gossip", talk about the events and describe behaviors that helped them to educate their children. The same way, men would gather for coffee or beer and used to state and evaluate village events, thus setting unwritten rules behavior and the knowledge base to solve problems.

In larger towns "events" come to us through the media, often accompanied by comments and judgments and here we take the information to assess situations and generate knowledge about our city and society.

But ... What if this information is distorted? The answer is simple, we will not know how to resolve the situation we face, let's see an example:

In some of the Juarez newspapers, you can see bodies of 2 men who were executed and sliced, then the events are followed by diatribe against the federal authorities bordering on despair and hatred against the "authorities".

In other words, two teenagers killed another two teens and butcher them, and somehow, it's President Calderón's fault... and people curse the president for the death and dismemberment of these people.

The information does the job reporting the death of these people and the media attacks whoever is NOT a sponsor.

But this information does not create knowledge since it's so distorted and manipulated. There are many questions that are not made because they are not "politically correct". So we will try to make a less phony analysis than the ones which are made on a daily basis by all the Juarez media.

We have some teenagers killing and butchering other human beings, but why? that's where the answers abound... duty for the narco, bounty by an enemy, being in a gang, etc.etc.

But what makes a teenager dispose of the life of another human being with such animal instinct? Who raised this young man/woman? How was his/her your childhood like? The peeping immediately fall to this level to the national and historical so called class struggle, "it's just that poverty, marginalization and inequality ... blah, blah, is what leads to crime."

But there has always been poverty and marginalization in Mexico and the world, more than half of the countries are even poorer than Mexico, and no such cases to be found. Since in Juarez, this phenomenon didn't exist a few years ago, but no one dares talk about these bastards, about the maquilas, encouragement of atheism and the chiefs of the people, about the landlords.

The maquila plan, developed according to the narrow interests of some owners of the town, without any real analysis, under the force of the landowner who only wanted to increase the price of their land and lease the real estates, justified by the creation of new jobs.

Unlike other countries where businesses that were yet to come had to be chosen to come and settle here; anyone who wanted to come here was more than welcome.

With the lure of cheap labor large companies came to settle and Juarez became a magnet for cheap labor across the country. Soon, truckloads of people looking for a job arrived and were crammed in small makeshift rooms the most wanted position was as a maquila operator. Then, women went to work in the maquila and soon the *droit de seigneur* took some interesting variations; Juarez took the shameful first place in single mothers and then, in underage girls in pregnancy.

No social infrastructure was made for the overall development of the workers, on the contrary, the people found a way to drunken people all day long, even though there's a schedule for selling alcohol; houses were turned into convenience stores, basically to sell beer and bars were turned into whorehouses to keep the wages of workers who were uprooted from their village ready for anything.

With Official support, bars became "table dances", strip clubs that offered better salaries for juarense girls who soon fell into prostitution and frequently into drug addiction as well.

In this scheme, large fortunes were made by those who transformed their rural land, industrial land, construction companies, beer tsars and drug tsars were made, everything was party while abandoned children grew alone in the neighborhood, in an absolute functional abandonment. While their mothers worked and had fun, some with an absent father, most wouldn't even know him.

The neighborhoods were nurtured porn, sex, beer, cheap music, drugs, gangs and children grew in the streets feeding on all this, compounded by the abuse of older kids, without a father figure, not an authority to teach them what is good and what is evil, without a corrective hand... and here they are, they're on the streets ready to kill anyone for a few pesos.

But the media does not dare to talk about this problem and most people are comfortable to say that the city has no choice. That the federation is to blame because they abandoned them and that they'll leave the city as soon as they can... but how can we reverse this tragedy? Who will dare attack the problem from its starting root? Will anyone face those who are to blame for the alcohol problems, the pornographers, or the picaderos?

Let's imagine that someone raises his voice and says remove porn from the TV!

The crowd will immediately yell, "You thick headed!" "Conservative!" "As if you pissed holy water!"

Or someone says mandatory childcare for all working mothers!

And the well-known answer, "are you crazy?" "Where are they going to get so many nurseries?"

Imagine someone saying "There will be no alcohol-sell on paydays, so you get a chance to actually take some money home".

He wouldn't even finish that sentence before having his ears explode!

Or what if someone proposed a parental neglect law and if any of the parents decide to abandon their children, they go to jail and the brats are forced to study or work.

Hitler! Mussolini! What more could they yell at someone who had that idea?

I do not even ask they closed for a time the tables, the picaderos, or the brothels.

You know? I think the best thing we can do is blame everything on President Calderón; of course, as long as we're not victims of a stray bullet, or as long as a stoned kid doesn't shot at us in order to carjack us, or as long as we don't get kidnap, or as long as extortionists don't burn down our business, or ... or ... or ... or ... or...

We are a society that have decided not solve our problems, that refuse to turn information into knowledge, and knowledge into solutions, "semos Mexas pues'n"

A new concept of solidarity in Juarez

Yesterday I attended the opening of a beautiful, elegant nursery, a playroom with guitars, hockey table, ping pong, a library with a large screen for watching movies and documentaries, with pc for children with wireless Internet, a sandpit and a few swings and slides in the elegant outdoors.

But this nursery has some very interesting features.

The idea and implementation is a PAN and the PRI is a major supporter and an inspiring priest.

The nursery is in a poor area in a public school and it'll be self-sustaining, it means that they will charge, mothers will donate one day's salary for maintenance of the nursery.

Mothers who work, will now go quietly to their jobs while their children are being cared for by specialists and in an atmosphere of games, fun and study. In past elections, I had the chance to interview Clara Torres, who had a good chance of being the first female mayor of Juarez, I asked her at that time:

- Clara, why do you want to be mayor? - To work for the children of Juarez - she answered emphatically and elaborated on her plans to support the Juarez's childhood.

Though she was more likely to win within the PAN candidates lost the primary election of her party and the PRI won the presidency.

Reyes Ferriz, PRI mayor, invites Clara Torres to be the director of kindergartens in the city, a second or third level position and the logic of power would say that someone who has been deputy, already had high positions nationwide, with many occupations in the private sector, including being a national equestrian champion, could hardly accept less in a government led by the opposite party, unless her desire to support children is greater than the whole political glamor, and so it was, yesterday she looked happy with the children and in her speech, she stressed that despite having different ideologies and belong to different parties, they both could work in coincidence for the good of the city.

Clara threatens to be building a nursery per month where it is the most needed and go knocking on doors to get the necessary funds for next year, because this year she has enough.

A very rare case amongst our politics.

Homecoming

Since last November you can appreciate an increase in the assistance of people to bars and restaurants. On Friday and Saturday it's quite hard to get a table. Real estate companies have declared the homecoming of some of the ones who left, which no doubt, represents good news.

But you know how your own memories can stab you on the back, sometimes they're just party-poopers, and it brings me back memories… a friend's wife who was left widowed, crying and sobbing over my murdered friend's coffin - but… "Why did we come back? We had already left".

Juarez needs its people, and even if leftists don't seem to agree with me, Juarez needs its entrepreneurs back. Juarez has no need for those who only want to profit with alcohol nor the so-called politicians. Juarez has a need for the people who actually provide goods and services to our society.

In this righteous circle of wealth generation, employment and support is given to thousands of people that came to these lands looking for a job, or looking for political asylum after being kicked out of the United States.

Lured by silver's heyday, they came all the way from Europe and other places around the world, entrepreneurs to the south of Chihuahua and they generated an economy in bloom. I see the book called, "El Parral de mis recuerdos", a book filled with pictures of bars and luxurious restaurants that had enormous shelves stacked with the best European wines, customers with tailored suits and fancy hats. This book talks about everyday stories written down about the abundance of employment, culture and fun. A bullfighting plaza, markets, theaters, factories, palaces, fancy farms and last but not least, about its mines.

A story tells that one time, the bishop came to visit the city and it was customary to greet him with a parade, in the bishop's honor. When the bishop saw the people he turned to look at the priest and said, "I came to visit the town's people, not the well-groomed".

So the priest replied, "Look sir, the one over there is the carpenter; the one wearing the frock-coat is the farmer; and the one on the far right is the butcher. The thing is sir, that here in Parral, people always like to dress up nicely". It was clear that the priest and the people were trying hard to look even better, but people could tell that the city was full of money at the moment.

But if all this money was able to lure entrepreneurs from around the world, it was also able to lure thugs. Quite often, the farms and the establishments would be robbed by bands of thieves. The most feared of them all, was Pancho Villa's.

In the beginning of 1910's genocide, also known as the Mexican Revolution, this band was hired by Hearst, a magnate from the U.S. newspapers, so they would fight against the Mexican government. So Villa was wrapped in a redeemer suit and was granted permission to kill.

Celia Herrera, witness, tells us on her book "Villa ante la Historia" the way that willa murdered, kidnapped, raped women and looted. The fifth horsemen and had unleashed hell over Parral, as the author states it.

Businessmen who weren't murdered, fled back to the U.S. or Europe. El Paso, TX, witnessed that gigantic immigration, quite similar to the one that's happening right now.

By the end of the revolution, the region was literally destroyed; factories had been turned into military headquarters; the ranches and farms had been completely destroyed; mines abandoned and the establishments all empty.

This should be a lesson for Juarez, it's not Calderon's war that created all these sicario kids. I believe it was the development program that we adopted. We sent women to work, we introduced them to alcohol, drugs and promiscuous sex, and now we ask ourselves, "why do they leave their children home alone?"

The maquiladoras from China are back as well and after hiring all the unemployed, they'll go back to hiring people from southern Mexico, who will all live in tiny rooms and surely will have a convenience store that will sell them beer late at night.

The "tables" or strip clubs will be the first ones to re-open, night clubs will start working again as well, where narcos will show off their well dressed women, their jewelry and head-turning cars; also, "decent places" run by narcos will re-establish. Everything will be back to normal, "no problem, bato".

Some philosophers say that blood that has been shed on the streets purifies its society. I would like to tell them that might be true, as long as there's a link between the real causes and an amendment to its errors. But in this case, I just can't see neither the cause nor the amendment.

Our town sages summarize it in one phrase, "it was Calderon's war".

Are we happy in Juarez?

A group of enthusiastic kids have a group on Facebook under the name "We are happy in Juarez", they share good "vibes", joy and good experiences, while reading, it came to mind about 10 years ago, when I arrived in Mexico City, they asked me: "What do you do in Juarez?" My answer was "to be happy".

What made me happy in Juarez? After watching the gray sky in DF, the blue sky seemed splendid to me, but nothing compared to the sunset where the sky seems to burn on a painting by Van Gogh. Or the night sky where the stars are so close and the moon shines wonderfully.

But mostly, going out at night to feel the "cool wind" with neighbors and hear anecdotes and everyday stories, that was the remembrance of when I was a child, in my beloved Parral, we sat on the floor in a circle to discuss stories and adventures until the bell rang, announcing it was 10 already, and our moms came out, at unison yelling us to get in.

I enjoyed greeting strangers as we crossed the street, the fluidity of its avenues, barbecues on Saturday with a beer and kind conversation of friends.

Ten years later I can't answer the same, I would like to join this Facebook group and say that we are happy, but how can I say I'm happy when remembering the face of my friend Carlos smiling, an image of his deformed face is superimposed by punches when we found him dead after his kidnapping, and how can I say I'm happy when I remember the painful stories of my friends deprived of freedom by humanoid beasts , how can I say that we are happy when the peace is gone and something as simple as answering the phone gets you in a defensive state because you can hear a voice that threatens you, how can I say we're be happy when you see how the savings of a lifetime are destroyed with your business closed.

But despite all these, people who seek happiness in Juarez are creditors to the largest of the cards by their attitude, their heroism and their temple, same thing with these entrepreneurs risking their lives by continuing opening their shops, factories, workshops, providing the services that people demand and paying wages that allow workers to live regardless of their risk.

It is true that there is a fight amongst drug gangs in our city, but not all crimes are committed by these bands, we made our nightmares come true, we fulfilled the failed promise of redemption of the poor, so much we promised them, so much we glorified them, that they got tired today and are willing to take what we told them it was theirs.

I've talked with criminals, I've asked them their reasons, I've read summaries of surveys of prisoners and there is not much difference between their motives and leftist discourses, "it's our turn", "let them have a lesson", "the raptor minority", "they have everything, and we don't".

The demagoguery of redemption of the poor which gave absolute power to the revolutionary class politics today is the motivation of criminals who want all the satisfactions that life can give them, bypassing the heavy process of working.

Sacred salaries, evil profits, good poor, evil rich, damned dogmas that political thieves planted in society and today take their toll, poverty and despair.

We are what we said we would be, why are we scared? Now let's say we'll be happy and maybe one day when they ask us again how we are doing in Juarez, we can say with a smile: HAPPY!

Epilogue

Today it seems that everything is back to normal in Juarez, after the triumph of PRI in federal elections, murders have declined dramatically and people return again. The semi deserted streets now look with heavy traffic, the tourism industry, elegant way of calling restaurants, bars, " tables" and brothels strongly supported by public resources reopen their doors.

The arrival of 10 maquiladoras is announced and after several years, new canvases asking workers are found in maquilas.

Businesses dare to reopen, abuses of local politicians and the police hide beneath the media under the guise of public bills "nothing happened here" we're ok".

It is true that the struggle for the ways of racking and drug market set the town on fire, but it is also true that it found tinder in a hedonistic society, lacking in universal values.

This subject's studies say that over 90% of criminals come from dysfunctional families, where the common denominator is the irresponsible father who abandons green fruit after he has bitten it.

From the mother who has to work or prostitute to survive and support her kids; from children left to the willing of the instincts of family or neighbors.

Looks like all that gore does not leave us any lesson, official charlatans blame Calderon for everything and now that he leaves, paradise comes back.

In a few decades we went from being a pious society to a depraved one. A teenager gave me in one sentence the description of Juarez: "No worries, man. This is modernity, do not be scared, bato."

Narcocorridos are still "trendy" in barbecues of the slums and it's not far-fetched the idea that in the future we have with golden letters in Congress the name of a famous assassin, such as with Villa.

Children continue watching with admiration the young men with brand new pickups accompanied by beautiful women, their AK-47, a bottle of whiskey and "dust", so the most common response, in this sector to the question of what do you want to be when you grow up? Sicario will be the answer.